Effective Document Management with SAP® DMS

SAP® Essentials

Expert SAP knowledge for your day-to-day work

Whether you wish to expand your SAP knowledge, deepen it, or master a use case, SAP Essentials provide you with targeted expert knowledge that helps support you in your day-to-day work. To the point, detailed, and ready to use.

SAP PRESS is a joint initiative of SAP and Galileo Press. The know-how offered by SAP specialists combined with the expertise of the Galileo Press publishing house offers the reader expert books in the field. SAP PRESS features first-hand information and expert advice, and provides useful skills for professional decision-making.

SAP PRESS offers a variety of books on technical and business related topics for the SAP user. For further information, please visit our website: *www.sap-press.com.*

Ulrich Schmidt, Gerd Hartmann
Product Lifecycle Management with SAP
2005, 617 pp.
978-1-59229-036-9

Michael Hölzer, Michael Schramm
Quality Management with SAP
2009, ~550 pp.
978-1-59229-262-2

Martin Murray
SAP MM: Functionality and Technical Configuration
2008, 561 pp.
978-1-59229-134-2

Eric Stajda

Effective Document Management
with SAP® DMS

Galileo Press

Bonn • Boston

ISBN 978-1-59229-240-0

© 2009 by Galileo Press Inc., Boston (MA)

1st Edition 2009

German Edition first published 2008 by Galileo Press, Bonn, Germany

Galileo Press is named after the Italian physicist, mathematician and philosopher Galileo Galilei (1564–1642). He is known as one of the founders of modern science and an advocate of our contemporary, heliocentric worldview. His words *Eppur si muove* (And yet it moves) have become legendary. The Galileo Press logo depicts Jupiter orbited by the four Galilean moons, which were discovered by Galileo in 1610.

Editor Meg Dunkerley
Copyeditor Jutta VanStean
Photo Credit Getty Images/Lawrence B. Aiuppy
Production Editor Kelly O'Callaghan
Cover Design Jill Winitzer
Layout Design Vera Brauner
Typesetting Publishers' Design and Production Services, Inc.
Printed and bound in Canada

To my wife, Liz.
Thank you for keeping the tea cup filled,
and for letting me know that I could do it.

Contents

4   Configuring SAP DMS 69

7   Frontends to SAP DMS 129

8   Integrating a CAD System to SAP DMS 143

9   Simple Document Approval Process using SAP Workflow 149

This chapter introduces you to SAP Document Management System (SAP DMS). It includes topics such as the benefits of SAP DMS, and how to use this book.

1   Introduction

In this chapter, you will learn about SAP DMS – what is it and what benefit can you expect to derive from an SAP DMS implementation? You will also learn about project complexity, and types of resources you should plan to have on your project. This chapter will also review how this book should be used, and is structured to progress from simple to complex topics. Finally, in this chapter, you will learn about the availability of SAP DMS in different releases of SAP software.

1.1   What Is SAP DMS?

SAP provides you with an enterprise document management system, SAP DMS, which you can use to manage documents for your business. Surprisingly, many companies are not aware this. This functionality is not part of an add-on or an additional piece of software you must purchase from SAP. Rather, it is part of your base SAP system. With a little basic knowledge on SAP DMS and its configuration, you can begin to take advantage of SAP DMS functionality in your system, such as the following:

- ▶ Secure storage for documents
- ▶ Check-in/check-out functionality
- ▶ Ability to classify documents for searching
- ▶ Linking of documents to other objects for visibility across the system
- ▶ Integration of Microsoft® Office applications for updating documents
- ▶ Elaborate security profiles to protect access to documents
- ▶ Controlling of documents through change management process

- Use of versions and revisions
- Full text search across stored documents
- Automatic conversion of documents to neutral format for viewing and long-term storage
- Integration of your CAD system into SAP DMS for management of drawings and models

This is a brief list of functionalities offered by SAP DMS. In this book, you will learn about all of these and much more.

1.2   Benefits of SAP DMS

There are many benefits to using SAP DMS, and a document management system in general. If you think about it, companies and individuals generate large numbers of documents each day. These documents are the lifeblood of a company. Without them, a company can't exist.

The documents could be stored on a person's laptop, or on a shared drive, or they could be hidden in someone's desktop drawer. People need access to these documents to make business decisions. Access to documents needs to be fast; people can't spend hours or days searching for the right information. This is where SAP DMS comes into play. Using it, you can take all of the key business documents your company is generating and store them in one place that everyone can use as the source. This is a major business benefit.

When implementing SAP DMS, you can expect to gain the following benefits to your business.

- Secure storage of documents
- Easy retrieval of documents
- Excellent search capabilities to cut down on time searching for documents
- A controlled environment for updates to documents
- Complex security rules to control access
- Increased visibility of key documents
- One source and one set of rules for managing documents

► Reduced time and effort spent on document management

► Ability to maintain document history to meet legal requirements

These are just a few of the possible business benefits of SAP DMS, and depending on your environment, you may have a completely different set of business challenges to solve and benefits to achieve. SAP DMS offers many benefits to all companies that own SAP software and generate documents. Implementing and using SAP DMS is therefore something every company should look into.

1.3   SAP DMS Project Complexity

In general, SAP DMS projects are not the most complex projects in the SAP world. They are not as complex as setting up finance or manufacturing, for example. In fact, they are typically light in terms of configuration and transactions. The complexity of an SAP DMS project will be driven by the number of different types of documents you want to manage, and by the rules for each document. As an example, in a complex project, you might want to manage all documents generated by your engineering, finance, and purchasing departments. Let's image that this means over 300 unique types of documents. For each unique document, you have to think about rules, such as: How do I want to search for the document? What is its lifecycle? What are the security rules? These are just a few rules that need to be defined.

In a simpler project, you might only want to manage documents coming from a customer and have them attached to the appropriate customer record in the SAP system. This is a simple and straightforward project because you are working on developing rules for only one type of document.

As mentioned previously, project complexity increases with the number of different types of documents to be managed.

1.4   Resources Required for a Project

An SAP DMS implementation project will require a varied set of resources, including the following:

► **Business users:** Business personnel who know about the rules for the documents that are being stored, such as who needs to approve a document before it becomes official. Business users will work with the SAP application consultant to map out a process for the documents being stored.

▸ **SAP application consultant:** The SAP application consultant works with business users to define a process for each document being stored. Once this process is defined, SAP application consultants map it to the SAP system and complete the SAP configuration.

▸ **SAP Basis/IT infrastructure resources:** The SAP Basis/IT infrastructure resources set up the infrastructure components required to support SAP DMS. This includes items such as content servers, cache servers, TREX, and conversion servers. Setting up the infrastructure components is usually one of the first activities accomplished in a project.

You may have one or several of each of these resource types, depending again on the number of documents you plan to store in the system.

1.5   How to Use This Book

As mentioned earlier, this book proceeds from simple to complex topics. In Chapter 2, you will start by answering some basic business questions, such as what types of documents you want to manage, and what attributes are associated with these documents. Answering these questions is important because it sets you up to start thinking about how your SAP DMS implementation will function. Chapter 3 reviews how to execute basic SAP DMS transactions, and step-by-step instructions are provided. Next, in Chapter 4, you will tackle how to configure the system. This means that you will learn how to set up items such as document types, additional attributes, and status networks. After you have completed the configuration, you can begin to use the system to store your documents.

The chapters that follow take you through more advanced topics such as defining and setting up security, infrastructure requirements, and the use of BAdIs or user exits to enhance the basic functionality provided by SAP.

The overall goal of the book is to prepare you for the implementation and use of SAP DMS in your environment. After reading this book and learning the material, you will not only have a thorough understanding of what SAP DMS is, but you will also be able to configure and use it effectively.

If you are a beginner with SAP DMS, it is best to proceed through the chapters as they are ordered. As mentioned previously, you will start with the simple and move to the complex, and each chapter will build on the knowledge you gained in the one before it. Advanced chapters assume that you have understood the content in the previous chapters. More advanced readers can start with the chapters they are interested in learning about. As an example, if you understand the SAP DMS transactions and configuration activities, but need information on how to set up SAP DMS security, you can go directly to the chapter that covers the topic of security.

1.6   A Note on the Availability of SAP DMS

SAP DMS is available in SAP R/3 3.1 and up. This book is written based on the SAP DMS functionality available in SAP ERP 6.0. This is a modern release; however, you will find most of the SAP DMS functionality described in this book available in much earlier releases of SAP R/3, such as 4.6 and 4.7. Therefore, you do not need to upgrade your system to the latest SAP release to take advantage of SAP DMS functionality. Most likely you can start working immediately using the release you have today.

1.7   Summary

In this chapter, we have provided a brief introduction to SAP DMS. You learned that through SAP DMS, SAP provides you with an enterprise document management system you can use without purchasing additional software. You then took a look at some of the benefits of implementing SAP DMS, including easy retrieval, secure storage, and the ability to apply complex security rules for document access. You were then given an idea of how to judge project complexity based on the number of different documents you plan to manage. You also learned about the three different types of resources required for an SAP DMS project: business users, SAP application consultants, and SAP Basis/IT infrastructure resources. Finally, you learned how to use this book, and about the general availability of SAP DMS across SAP software releases.

In the next chapter, Chapter 2, you will identify questions you need to answer before starting your SAP DMS project.

This chapter reviews information you need to address before starting your SAP DMS project. This is the foundation to making sure your project will be successful.

2 Questions to Answer before Starting Your SAP DMS Project

Before starting your SAP DMS project, there are a number of questions you need to answer, and considerations that you should take into account. At this point in the process, you should be focused on defining your requirements and goals, and not so much on what the SAP DMS system can do. After you prepare a solid foundation and plan, the information can be used effectively when you begin configuring and using the SAP DMS system.

Defining your requirements and goals is critical to project success. It's much easier to reach a goal efficiently with planning and insight. This chapter discusses the basic considerations you need to address before starting your SAP DMS project.

2.1 Defining which Documents to Manage with SAP DMS

The first step in your SAP DMS project is defining the documents you want to manage. On a daily basis, a business can generate thousands of documents, which make up the intellectual capital and value of that business. Some generated documents are trivial, whereas others are critical to the production and sale of products. Critical documents include CAD drawings, test reports, product specifications, product literature, and financial documents. Without these critical documents, a company can't create, purchase, or sell goods. These are the types of documents that should be managed within SAP DMS.

If a company is using SAP software, it is most likely that business processes such as manufacturing, sales, purchasing, engineering, and finance are being executed and managed within the SAP system. When selecting which documents to manage within SAP DMS, you should select documents that support such business processes. Key documents are then gathered into one location where the business process is being executed. This makes the data more widely available, less difficult to find, and updates can be managed in a controlled manner.

> **Example**
>
> You want to manage all documents associated with the engineering change process you execute within the SAP system. Multiple documents are generated and controlled through this process, and these documents should be stored within SAP DMS.

2.2 How Documents Fit Into the Overall Business Process

The next important step is defining how the documents you want to manage fit into the overall business process with which they are associated. Are documents created or required at certain steps in the process? Which business objects are documents associated with? Map out your business in a process flow. For each step in the flow, you can identify which documents are required. You should look at what is significant about each document and what it feeds downstream or what it triggers.

As an example, it is a best practice that each company has a process for the development and introduction of new products. During this process, certain documents are required to move to the next phase or maturity level of the product design. If you are in the "prototype" phase of your product design, you will need drawings released at a certain status, signifying that they can be used to build prototypes but not production parts. Along with the drawings, you may need documents such as specifications and finite elements analysis reports.

> **Example**
>
> Imagine that you work for a company that produces bicycles. Before a bicycle can be shipped from the factory, a document describing how the bicycle should be assembled by the consumer must be stored in the system, printed, and included as part of the overall package.
>
> The assembly instructions are related to the finished good item material master for the bicycle in the SAP system, and may be included as an item in the bill of materials (BOM). You might also have a business process or system check in place to make sure that the assembly instructions are stored in the SAP system before manufacturing and shipping of the bicycle can happen.

2.3 How to Search for Stored Documents

With SAP DMS you are not just storing files or attachments. Along with the files, you are also storing attributes. Examples of standard attributes stored with each file include the following:

▶ Description

▶ Owner

▶ Responsible lab office

Along with standard attributes you can store additional attributes, which can be used to search for stored documents.

For example, if you are storing CAD drawings you might want to know in which CAD application and release of the application the drawings were created. You might also want to know the size of the drawing, and which customers are using it. These are a few examples of additional attributes you might want to maintain.

This is an important topic, and you should make the necessary effort to define and add document attributes that are required to fulfill your search requirements. This will prevent you from creating an unstructured and unsearchable system.

Example

You plan on storing the resumes of all of your employees. When new positions or opportunities become available, you want to be able to search across the resumes to find qualified internal candidates, using the following attributes:

▶ Employee location

▶ Salary category (hourly, salaried)

▶ Willing to relocate

▶ Skill set

▶ Languages spoken

▶ Education level

Searching on the above attributes will return a list of resumes that match the selection criteria.

Beyond searching on attributes, SAP DMS also offers you the capability to perform full text searches on stored documents. This functionality is provided via the Index Server, which is a component of the SAP Knowledge Provider.

2.4 Define the Lifecycle of Documents

Each document can have a lifecycle of its own. Think of a lifecycle as the time from which the document was created to when it is obsolete. Steps in between can include times when the document is in one of the following states:

- In work
- Pending approval
- Approved
- Released

At each step of the lifecycle, the SAP system can be configured to act in a certain way or perform certain actions, such as sending notifications when a document reaches the released state.

> **Example**
>
> When a document is in the state "released," you can specify that no further updates can be made to the document without creating a new version. The released version remains as history in the system. Imagine that the released version relates to a certain design or release level of a product you are building. Because it remains as history in the system, you can always track back to the documentation that was used to build the product at that specific design or release level.

2.5 The Change Control Process

Another item you need to address and plan for before implementing SAP DMS is the change control process. That is, for documents being stored, you need to determine whether updates are controlled through a change control process. A change control process could involve that changes to a document are controlled through the SAP Engineering Change Management in the SAP system. This is a formal and rigorous process that can include capturing a reason for changes, elements of workflow, and required digital signatures for release. A formal change control process provides you with a complete history of when and why a document was updated. This is important for documents that are critical to business operation.

As an example, let's take the case of CAD drawings again. Manufacturing is dependent on these drawings to build the product in a correct manner. If there is no change process in place for these drawings, someone could update them at will and never communicate the changes. As a result, the engineering group might have one idea of how the product looks, and manufacturing might have another, different idea. A business can't operate in such a manner for any amount of time.

2.6   A Formal Approval Process

Before a document can become an official released version, does it have to go through a formal approval process? It depends. Typically, documents that are critical to the design and manufacturing of a product, such as CAD drawings, specifications, and design failure mode effects analysis, go through a formal approval process. This process can be facilitated through a workflow process, and might require a digital signature. With a digital signature, the user is required to input their username and password or other type of security information to validate that they are signing off on or are approving the document. The result of the formal approval is a released version of the document with a record of who approved it. Any further changes to the document can be made only by creating a new version.

> **Example**
>
> When a document reaches the status of "review," a workflow process is started that sends a workflow notification to a reviewer. The reviewer reviews the document and decides if it should be released or sent back for rework. If the person decides that the document needs rework, he will put the document back into a status of "in work" and provides appropriate commentary back to the person who requested the review. If approved, the document is set to a status of "released" and is locked to prevent further change. For additional changes to the document, a new version must be created. The released version remains in the system as history.

2.7   Security Requirements

Next, you need to address security requirements for each document. What roles in the business are allowed to change each document? Does the document status need to be taken into consideration? For example, when a document is in "in work," should a select group be able to view it? When the document is released, should it be opened for everyone to view?

For example, all CAD drawings are viewable by everyone after they are released for production. A "released for production" design means that the manufacturing group is building a production product and that product is being sold to the consumer. Therefore, the design can be deconstructed and analyzed. Before a design is released for production, while in a "prototype" or "early development" stage, only the project team that is working on the design has access to view or change the drawings. This reduces the possibility of design secrets getting out before the product is released.

The SAP system provides a complex set of conditions you can use to control access to documents. Several conditions can be combined, including document type, status, and authorization group assigned to the document.

> **Tip**
>
> You can set up the SAP DMS system so that, for example, only a person in the role of "Document Control" under project "F1100" can view documents that are in a status of "Pending Review." After this is done, no other roles will have access.

2.8   Defining which Type of Application Files to Store

Defining the type of application files to be stored within SAP DMS is important. The term *application file* is defined as the output file of a specific application. Sample applications include Microsoft Word, Excel®, and PowerPoint®. Each application can be configured in the SAP system to behave in a certain manner when an associated file is launched for display or change.

To define the appropriate application file types, take a look around your business and see what applications are being used. Most likely it is a basic set of applications. The SAP system does not restrict to the type of application files that can be stored. Therefore, it is possible to store the output of just about any application in SAP DMS.

2.9   Versions and Revisions

What do the terms version and revision mean to your business, and how are they used? When working with SAP DMS, you can use both. A *version* in SAP DMS is defined as a separate instance of a document information record that has its own status, such as "in work" or "released." It is a snapshot in time. A *revision* level is assigned to a document version and is associated with a release state. It is usually used as a representation of a major change. For each document, you can store multiple versions. With each version, you can assign a revision identifier.

It is important to clarify what these terms mean to your business, because they can become confusing. When you start to work with the system and start to speak of versions and revisions, each person may have a different picture in mind, because at times, the terms are interchangeable.

For example, you might create a document and store it in SAP DMS. On storing, an initial version of 00 is assigned to the document. Let's say you then decide that you want to save your work as a snapshot at version 00. To do so, you can create a new version of the document, to which version 01 is assigned. When your work on version 01 of the document is complete, you want to release this as an official revision of the document. You can release the document through a change control process that associates revision A to version 01. The "revision" indicator identifies to your business users that the document is an officially released document. Further changes will be made to version 02 of the document, and it may take many additional versions until a revision B is created.

2.10   Searching and Maintenance in Multiple Languages

You should also consider whether you will need to maintain certain attributes, such as "description," in multiple languages. This requirement is not uncommon in large companies that have locations and employees across the globe with business transactions performed in multiple languages. For such situations, the SAP system provides you with the capability to maintain entry, display, and searching of attributes in multiple languages. It is a good idea to plan for this up front, because you will need to take this into consideration when you are configuring the SAP system.

2.11   Stored Document Volume and Size

It is good to have an upfront idea of the volume of documents to be stored. The infrastructure, and specifically the content server, will need to be sized differently to support, for example, ten thousand or ten million documents.

Also, understanding the average size of files being stored will help with network sizing. Document consumers will likely exist in a number of different geographic locations. Depending on where content servers are located, users viewing or changing documents stored in SAP DMS will be accessing files across a wide area network. This will impact wide area network usage and sizing.

Example

At your company, the creators of CAD data are located in the Detroit office. This is also the location where the content server is located. The CAD data can be between 10MB and 35MB per file.

Individuals using the CAD data are located across the globe, including at locations in Europe and Asia. Each time an individual from Europe or Asia views the CAD data, it is accessed across the wide area network and downloaded to the local PC. Because the files are very large, this can have a major impact on wide area network utilization and on the time spent waiting for the document by the user. To address this, you can install a cache server at the different remote locations. Data is then cached at the remote site the first time it is viewed. Additional requests by individuals at the remote location will first go the cache server to see if documents can be accessed there, and only if this is not possible, go to the remote content server. If files can be pulled from the cache server, response times for delivering the files to users will be quicker and the impact on the performance of the wide area network will be decreased.

2.12 Locations for Document Creators vs. Consumers

It is also best to identify the different geographic locations of creators and consumers of documents. A *creator* is someone who generates and stores documents in the system. A *consumer* is someone who searches for documents and displays them. If there are a large number of document creators at a specific location, such as at an engineering center, the site could require the installation of a local content server. At locations with a high number of document consumers, such as manufacturing plants, it might be beneficial to install a cache server. Following these two concepts will help decrease the impact on the performance of your wide area network.

2.13 Document Retention Requirements

Document retention requirements define how long a document should be stored or available based on business and legal requirements. Therefore, you need to review what your retention requirements are, per document.

For example, in the construction industry it is considered a best practice to retain all construction drawings and specifications for an indefinite period. Also, studies and reports that relate to a building's design must be maintained indefinitely.

It is also best to address how a document should be handled after the retention period has passed. That is, you need to decide whether it should be archived or deleted. Considering document retention requirements is important mainly because the system must support the legal requirements of the business. If a lawsuit is brought forward against your company, you must be able to produce documents that support your case. In the case of product liability law suits, not being able to produce proper documentation can lead to catastrophic results.

Example

Your company has decided that it will keep all CAD data related to a product's design for a total of fifteen years after the start of the product's production. When this period has been passed, all CAD data will be deleted from the system if the product is no longer being manufactured. To accomplish this, a process runs daily in the SAP system to see if any documents have passed the retention period. If so, they are marked for deletion. Then, using a different process, documents are permanently deleted from the system.

2.14 Conversion to Neutral Format for Long Term Retention

For long term retention, documents can be converted from their original application file format to a neutral file format such as TIF or PDF. If document retention requirements are that a document should be kept for the next twenty years, it is almost certain that the application the file was originally created in will no longer function at that point in the future. "Neutral" file formats such as TIF and PDF help solve this problem.

Example

On the release of product and packaging specifications stored in SAP DMS, all associated files are converted from the original Word format to the PDF format. This conversion is carried out automatically by the SAP system when the status of "released" is reached. The trigger for the conversion is controlled through SAP implementation guide (IMG) configuration and carried out on a conversion server, which is a component of the SAP Knowledge Provider.

2.15 Summary

In this chapter, we have reviewed important issues you need to address before an SAP DMS implementation. It is important that you define your goals and prepare for moving into the next steps of your SAP DMS project: using and configuring the system.

It is therefore best to have answers to the following questions:

- What documents do you want to manage with SAP?
- How do documents fit into the overall business process?
- How do you want to search for documents?
- What is the change control process?
- Is there a formal approval process?
- What are the security requirements?
- What type of application files will be stored?
- How are versions and revisions used in your business?
- Do you need to support searching and maintenance in multiple languages?
- What is the volume and size of documents to be stored?
- Are there document retention requirements?
- Do documents need to be converted to a neutral format for long term retention?

The more clearly you can answer these questions, the more successful your project will be in the long run.

In the next chapter, Chapter 3, you will learn how to execute basic SAP DMS transactions and other functions.

This chapter presents instructions you need to execute SAP DMS and other related transactions.

3   SAP DMS Step-by-Step Instructions

In this chapter you will learn how to execute SAP DMS and related transactions. This will include transactions to create, change, display, and search for document information records. You will also learn about ancillary transactions such as the product structure browser and classification search. It is important to have a good understanding of how the transactions covered in this chapter operate before proceeding with the configuration activity. Spending time executing these transactions will make learning and understanding the configuration process much easier.

3.1   SAP DMS Transactions

In Table 3.1, you will find the SAP DMS and related transactions that will be demonstrated in this chapter. You will be given step-by-step instructions for executing each transaction. These are the main transactions you need to focus on learning.

SAP Transaction	Description
CV01N	Create Document
CV02N	Change Document
CV03N	Display Document
CV04N	Find Document
CC04	Product Structure Browser
CL30N	Find Document In Class

Table 3.1 SAP DMS and Related Transactions

3.2   Transaction CV01N - Creating a Document Information Record

The first thing you will learn in this chapter is how to create a document information record. This is the beginning of creating an SAP DMS system; all other actions follow this action. You are initiating the record in the system, after which you can carry out the display, and change actions, as well as many other actions.

3.2.1   Execute Transaction CV01N (Create Document)

On the initial screen, the first item you need to concern yourself with is selecting the document type. For this exercise, select DOCUMENT TYPE DRW (Eng./Des. Drawing). This is the standard document type delivered by SAP. The document type is a high-level classification of what type of document you will be creating. It drives items such as status network, additional attributes, security, and other rules.

As shown in the screen in Figure 3.1, you can also enter a DOCUMENT NUMBER, DOCUMENT PART, and DOCUMENT VERSION. However, for this exercise, do not enter any values into these fields. The SAP system will automatically assign correct values based on how this document type is configured. This configuration will be explained in the chapter on how to configure the SAP DMS system.

When you have entered the DOCUMENT TYPE, press Enter to move to the next screen.

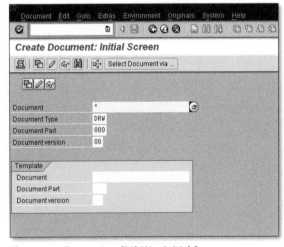

Figure 3.1   Transaction CV01N – Initial Screen

3.2.2 Fill Out Relevant Fields on the Document Data Tab

You must now fill out the relevant fields on the DOCUMENT DATA tab of the document information record. This includes DESCRIPTION, LAB OFFICE, CHANGE NUMBER, and AUTHORIZATION GROUP. A short description of each field on this tab is provided in Table 3.2.

Field	Description
DESCRIPTION	A short description of the document information record.
DOCUMENT STATUS	The current status of the document information record. When configuring a document type, an initial document status will usually be set. In this case, it is WR (WORK REQUEST).
CM RELEVANCE	Indicates if the object is controlled by Configuration Management.
USER	The person responsible for the document information record.
LAB OFFICE	The office or area of the business to which the document information record belongs.
CHANGE NUMBER	If the document is under change control, the number of the engineering change master is entered here.
AUTHORIZATION GROUP	The authorization group to which the document belongs. This field helps drive security.
SUPERIOR DOCUMENT	Helps determine a hierarchy. When assigned, you can display a simple document structure.
ORIGINALS	Area where you attach original files to the document information record.

Table 3.2 Description of Fields on the Document Data Tab

For this exercise, enter a DESCRIPTION and select a LAB OFFICE. Leave the other fields in the DOCUMENT DATA and SUPERIOR DOCUMENT areas as they are.

Adding Long Text

In this example, we are entering a short description for the document information record. You can enter a longer description by clicking on the CREATE LONG TEXT button next to the DESCRIPTION field. This lets you enter an unlimited amount of text that describes the document information record.

3.2.3 Add an Original File

Next, you need to add an original file to the document information record. You accomplish this by clicking on either the CREATE ORIGINAL or OPEN ORIGINAL button on the ORIGINALS toolbar, as circled in Figure 3.2. Select a Microsoft Word or Excel file, or a text file, from your desktop. After you select a file, you will be asked to associate it to an application. If you selected a Word file, you will want to associate it to the application type DOC or WRD. The application controls how the file is changed or displayed.

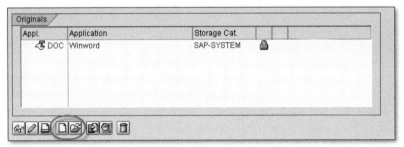

Figure 3.2 Buttons to Add Original Files

3.2.4 Check in an Original File

When you check in an original file into secure storage, it is stored back into the SAP database. As shown in Figure 3.3, you can click on the button CHECK IN ORIG. on the Originals toolbar. On the screen that appears, you need to select SAP DB as the storage data. Next, you need to select a storage category of SAP-SYSTEM. After making your selections, click on the green checkmark to continue. You will notice that the padlock symbol next to the original file is closed. This signifies that the file needs to be checked in. The actual movement of the file from your local system to the secure storage occurs when you save the document information record.

3.2.5 Fill Out Attributes on the Additional Data Tab

The ADDNL DATA tab contains attributes that help further define the document information record. The attributes appear on this tab because of the association of a default class to the document type during configuration. The class is defined using the SAP Classification functionality and contains a definition for each attribute, including values and whether a specific attribute is required. Further information on setting up a class will be covered in the configuration chapter, Chapter 4.

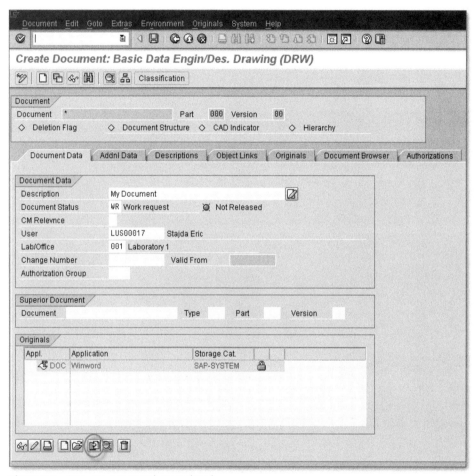

Figure 3.3 Document Data Tab Completed

The additional attributes are important because they are used to later search for the document information record. This is a topic of great importance because one of the goals of having a document management system is the ability to search and locate documents quickly. A good deal of effort should be put into defining what additional attributes a user will be required to populate.

For this exercise, the document type DRW has three additional attributes:

- ► FORM SIZE
- ► DATA CARRIER
- ► LINE NUMBER

Select a value from the value list associated with each attribute, as shown in Figure 3.4.

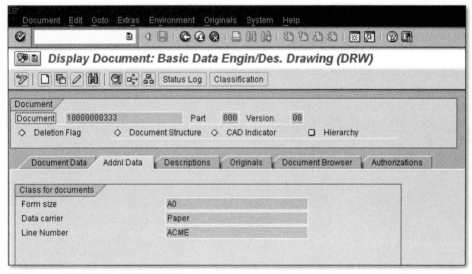

Figure 3.4 Addnl Data Tab Filled Out

3.2.6 Add a Language-Dependent Description

It is possible to maintain multiple language-dependent descriptions for the document information record. This means that if a user logs into the SAP GUI with a different language, for example French, they will be presented with the French description of the document information record if it is maintained.

Maintenance of language-dependent descriptions is done on the DESCRIPTIONS tab. For our exercise, select this tab and enter the French description for the document information record by selecting the language FR and entering the description MOI DOCUMENT, as shown in Figure 3.5.

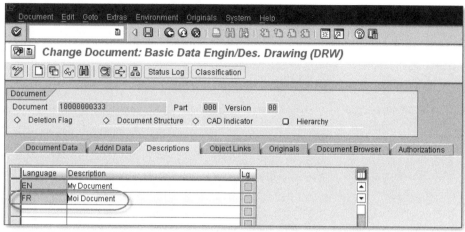

Figure 3.5 French Language-Dependent Description Added

3.2.7 Link the New Document to Another SAP Object

On the OBJECT LINKS tab, you can link a document information record to another object or record in the SAP system. Using object links is important because they allow you to connect a document information record to the supporting business object. This helps cut down on time spent searching for the relevant documentation.

> **Example**
>
> A customer has sent a set of documents that define the requirements associated with bidding on projects and doing business together. These documents will be stored in SAP DMS. When they are stored, each document should be linked to the SAP customer record for that customer. Doing so will make each document accessible from the SAP customer record. Therefore, whoever looks at this record will not need to do a lot of searching to find documents that list requirements for bidding on projects and doing business with this customer.

Table 3.3 shows the object links that are possible with document type "DRW." Defining which objects a document record can be linked to will be covered in the next chapter.

Object Links To Other SAP Objects		
Asset Master	General Notification	Production Versions
BOM Header	HR Master Link	Purchase Order Item
BOM Item	iPPE Variant	Purchase Req. Item
Change Number	Material Master	Quality Notification
Claim	Measuring Points	Reference Location
Class	Network Activity	Sales Document Item
cProjects Element	Object Link	SAP-EIS:Master Data
Customer	Plant Material	Vendor
Document Information Record	PPE Node	WBS Element
Equipment Master	Prod. Resource/Tool	
Functional Location	Production Order	

Table 3.3 Object Links Possible with Document Type "DRW"

When you link a document information record to another SAP Object, that document information record becomes visible in the corresponding transactions for that object. As illustrated in Figure 3.6, you will link the document information record you are creating to a material master. To do this, on the OBJECT LINKS tab, select the tab MATERIAL MASTER. In the field MATERIAL, search for a material to link to. Any material master will do for this demonstration.

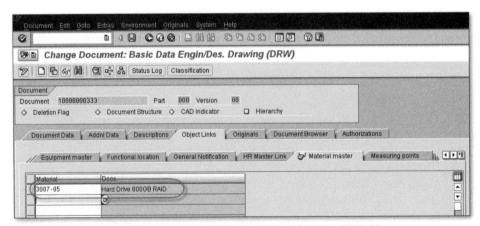

Figure 3.6 Document Information Record Linked to Material Master 3007-05

After the document information record is saved, you will able to open the linked material master through the change material transaction (MM02) and see the link between the document information record and the material master, as shown in Figure 3.7.

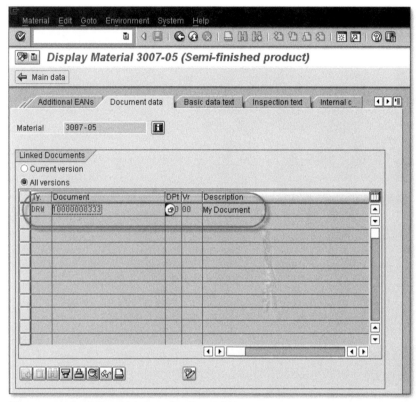

Figure 3.7   The Object Link from the Material Master

3.2.8   Save the Document Information Record

At this point, all of the required data has been entered for the document information record. You can now save the document information by clicking on the Save icon. Saving will initiate multiple actions:

1. Original files associated during the creation process will be moved from the local system into SAP.

2. A document number, part, and version will be assigned to the document information record.

On saving, as shown in Figure 3.8, you are returned to the initial creation screen showing the assigned document number, type, part, and version.

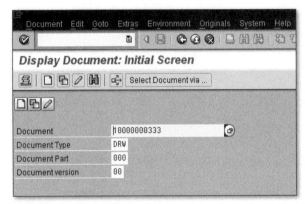

Figure 3.8 A Saved Document Information Record with Number, Type, Part, and Version Assigned

The creation process is now complete and the document information record has been created in the SAP System. You can now move on to the change process. This is the next logical step in the learning process.

3.3 Transaction CV02N - Changing a Document Information Record

Using Transaction CV02N (Change Document), you can now change the document information record you created earlier. Actions performed when changing a document information record might include the following:

- ▶ Update basic or additional attributes
- ▶ Change the document status
- ▶ Add additional objects links
- ▶ Creating a new version of the document information record
- ▶ Change an original file
- ▶ Add another original file

You will learn how to perform all of these using the step-by-step instructions that follow.

3.3.1 Execute the Transaction CV02N (Change Document)

On the initial screen of Transaction CV02N (Change Document), select the document you want to change. For this exercise, use the document information record you created previously and enter the document number, type, part, and version. If you do not remember the document number, use the PROCESSED DOCUMENTS button, circled in the toolbar in Figure 3.9, to locate document information records that you have previously worked on.

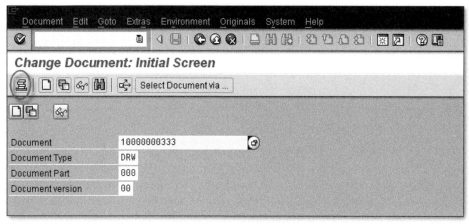

Figure 3.9 Selecting a Document Information Record to Change using the Processed Documents Button

After the document number, type, part, and version have been specified, press ⌜Enter⌝ to open the document information record in change mode.

3.3.2 Update the Description Field and Lab Office

With the document information record in change mode, you can now make changes. For our exercise, update the DESCRIPTION field and change the LAB/OFFICE to which the document information record belongs.

All changes made are recorded in the change history of the document information record. Displaying the change history will be covered later in this chapter when we look at executing the transaction to display a document information record.

3.3.3 Change the Status of the Document Information Record

The current status of your document is WR or WORK REQUEST. Change the document status to IW or IN WORK. To do this, select the DOCUMENT STATUS field and execute the search help (F4). As shown in Figure 3.10, the list of statuses that can be set appears. From the list, select IW.

When setting this status, a screen will pop up asking you to make a status log entry. This is meant to be a short description to document the status change. It will be recorded in the status log and will be accessible by clicking on the STATUS LOG button.

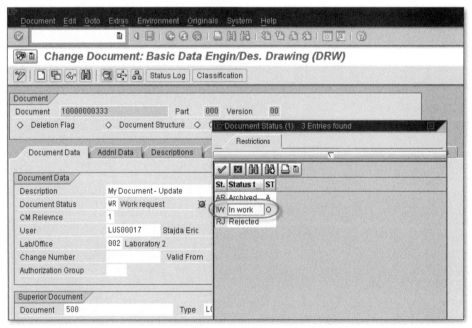

Figure 3.10 Selecting the Document Status

The document status represents where the document is at in its status network. A *status network* represents the lifecycle of the document information record. Each document type can have its own associated status network. Setup of a status network is covered in the chapter on configuration, Chapter 4.

3.3.4   Add Object Links

When changing a document information record, you can add object links. For this exercise, link the document information record to a second material master. Or, if your system has customer information, link it to a customer. This demonstrates that it is possible to include additional object links. This is useful when the document information record is related to many different objects, because it makes it visible on those objects.

3.3.5   Save the Document Information Record

All changes to be made to the document information record are now complete. Save the document information record. You will be returned to the main screen of the change document transaction.

3.3.6   Create a New Version of the Document Information Record

To demonstrate another key capability, you will now create a new version of the document information record. This will be version "01". Version "00" will remain as it was last saved and because it is not released or locked, it is still possible to make changes to this version. The important concept to understand is that you now have two versions of the document information record. The document information records are still related, but each version could have its own original files, settings for attributes, or objects links.

To create a new version of the document information record, click on the NEW VERSION button circled in Figure 3.11. You will be prompted to confirm that you want to create the new version based on version 00. Click on the CONTINUE button. You will then be asked if you would like to also copy the object links. This means that the new version will be linked to the same object as version 00. Confirm that you want to copy the objects links. You will then be placed into change mode for version 01 of the document information record.

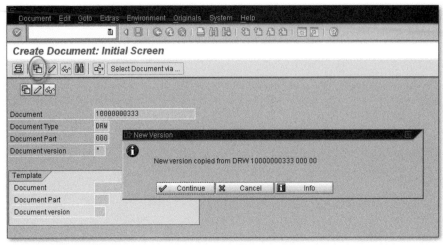

Figure 3.11   Creating a New Version of a Document Information Record

3.3.7   Check Out the Original File Associated with the New Version

Another important concept is changing an original file associated with a document information record. When you created the document information record, you associated an original file. This was a Word, Excel, or other type of file. When the new version of the document information record was created, the original files were also copied to the new version. You will now make changes to the original file associated with version 01 of the document information record. Afterwards, you should take a look at the original file associated with version 00 of the document information record and note how they differ. The version 00 original files will not have the changes you made to the original files in version 01.

To change an original file, highlight the file in the ORIGINALS area of the DOCUMENT DATA tab and click on the CHANGE ORIGINAL button, as circled in Figure 3.12.

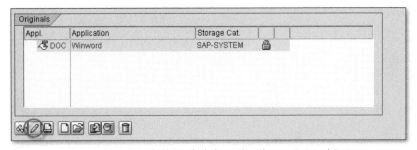

Figure 3.12   Select the Original File and Click on the Change Original Button

You will be prompted to provide a location on your local system where the original file will be checked out to, as shown in Figure 3.13. The default path is where the original file was checked in from, but you can specify a different path. After the checkout location has been selected, click on the CONTINUE button. The file is then opened in the appropriate application for updating. For this exercise, if your original file is a Word file, Word will open and you can make your changes.

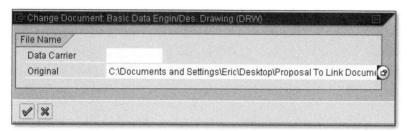

Figure 3.13 Select a Local Storage Location to which to Check Out the File

For now, updates you are making are on a local copy of the original file. Other users can still access the original file to display it. When they do so, they access the latest copy that was stored in the SAP system. They can also see that the file is out for modification; the padlock icon is unlocked when a file is checked out, as shown in Figure 3.14.

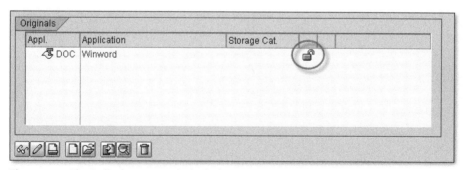

Figure 3.14 The Padlock Icon Is Unlocked when an Original File Is Checked Out

Make your updates to the original file and save the file. Close the application in which you were making changes.

3.3.8 Check in the Original File after Changes

After completing your changes, you need to check the original file back in. This will move the original file, with changes, from your local system back into the secure storage, making the updates you made accessible to other users.

When you checked out the original file for change, the system exited you from change mode on the document information record. To check in the original file, you need to open the document information record in change mode again. To check in the original file, highlight the original file and click on the CHECK IN ORIG. button, as shown in Figure 3.14. After doing so, the padlock icon will once again lock, and the storage category will be populated. The actual movement of the file from your local system to the secure storage occurs when you save the document information record.

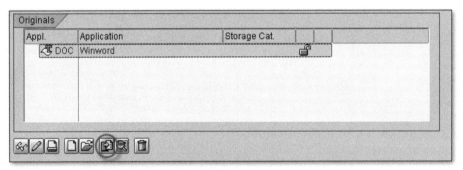

Figure 3.15 Check in the Original File after Making Changes

3.3.9 Add Another Original File to the New Version

You can have multiple original files associated with a document information record. To demonstrate this, open version 01 of the document information record you have been working on and add another original file. Save the document information record.

The change process is now complete. You can next move on to the display process.

3.4 Transaction CV03N - Displaying a Document Information Record

Using Transaction CV03N (Display Document), you can display the document information record you created earlier. When displaying a document information record, you can review a variety of information. In this section, you will go through step-by-step instructions for displaying key information. Keep in mind that it is also possible to review much of this information during the creation or change process.

Key items you might want to review when displaying a document information record include the following:

▸ An original file

▸ The status network

▸ The change history for the document information record

▸ The number of versions of the document information record

3.4.1 Display an Original File Associated with the Document Information Record

Using transaction CV03N, open one of the document information records you created during the previous exercises. Double-click on one of the original files, or select the original file and click on the DISPLAY ORIGINAL button. The original file will be opened in its corresponding application.

3.4.2 Display the Status Network

Each document type will have a status network associated to it. As mentioned previously, the status network represents the lifecycle of the document information record. A simple example of a status network is that a document information record starts in the status of IN WORK. At some point in time, a review needs to take place and the document information record is set to a status of IN REVIEW. After the review is held, and if everything is ok, the document information record status is set to RELEASED. This is the final state.

To display the status network for a document information record, follow the menu path EXTRAS • DISPLAY STATUS NETWORK. As shown in Figure 3.16, a pop-up screen appears with a graphical display of the status network.

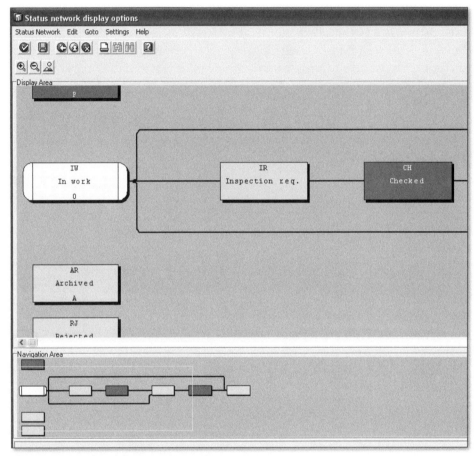

Figure 3.16 Display of the Status Network

You will notice that statuses display in yellow, green, or red. The color yellow represents the current status of the document information record. Green represents statuses that can be set. Red means that you cannot set these statuses based on the current status of the document information record.

3.4.3 Review the Change History for the Document Information Record

It is important to be able to view the change history for a document information record. To have a controlled system, you need to know three basic elements: who has changed the data, when was the data changed, and what specifically was changed. SAP software excels at capturing this type of information.

To display the change history for the document information record, follow the menu path ENVIRONMENT • DISPLAY CHANGES, the result of which is shown in Figure 3.17.

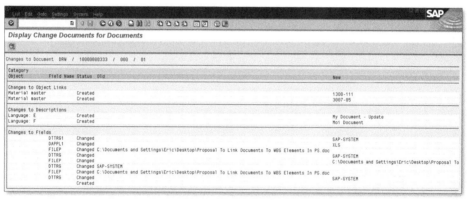

Figure 3.17 The Change History for a Document Information Record

The change history report is broken down into multiple sections, which include changes to objects, descriptions, and fields. As mentioned previously, with each change, you can find out who made the change, when the change was made, and what was changed.

3.4.4 Check How Many Versions are Available for a Document Information Record

When reviewing a document information record, it is important to be able check whether other versions of the document information record are available. For example, someone might have created a new version and might be in the process of making updates. You can check whether other versions of the document information record are available by following the menu path EXTRAS • VERSIONS. As shown in Figure 3.18, you can see the other available versions of the document information record and the current status of those versions. You can open a version of the document information record by selecting and double–clicking it.

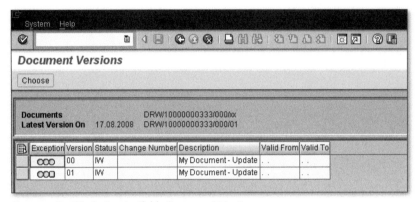

Figure 3.18 Displaying Available Document Versions

The display process is now complete. You can next move on to searching for the document information records you have created.

3.5 Transaction CV04N - Searching for a Document Information Record

Now that you have mastered the basic concepts of creating, changing, and displaying document information records, you will next learn about searching for them. One of the key capabilities and benefits of implementing SAP DMS is the ability to search for what has been stored, and the search transaction allows you to find the proverbial needle in the haystack. Without search capabilities, you would only have a bunch of documents stored in a secure system, which would be no better than having the documents stored on a shared drive somewhere, or placed in a folder on your desk.

Using Transaction CV04N (Find Document), you can search for documents using a variety of methods. This includes searching by the following:

▶ Basic document attributes

▶ Additional attributes or classification

▶ Object links

▶ Texts or long text

▶ Full text

As shown in Figure 3.19, each method relates to a different tab in the FIND DOCU-MENT transaction. You are not limited to searching by a single method or tab at a time; if you want, you can mix and match different methods. A sample search that mixes methods would be to find all document information records of type "DRW" that have the word "Pump" in their description. To execute this search you need to enter search criteria on the DOCUMENT DATA (*) and TEXTS tabs.

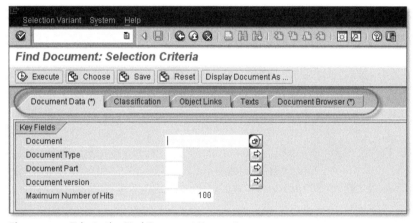

Figure 3.19 Tabs in the Find Document Transaction

3.5.1 Search for a Document Information Record using Document Type and User as the Criteria

In our first search example, you will learn how to search by document type and user. This is a simple example to get you acquainted with the use of the Find Document transaction.

The goal of our search is to find all document information records of type "DRW." This will locate all of the document information records you created earlier in this chapter.

As shown in Figure 3.20, as search criteria enter "DRW" in the DOCUMENT TYPE field, and then enter your user name in the USER field. Click on the EXECUTE button to start the search.

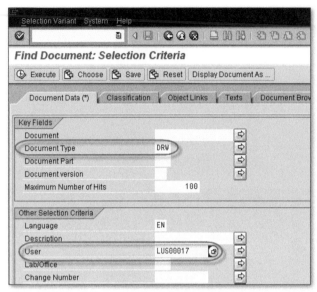

Figure 3.20 Search Criteria to Locate Document Information Records by Type and User

As shown in Figure 3.21, the document information records matching the search criteria are returned. You can double-click on a document information record in the list to open the record. From here, you can proceed with updating the document information record if required.

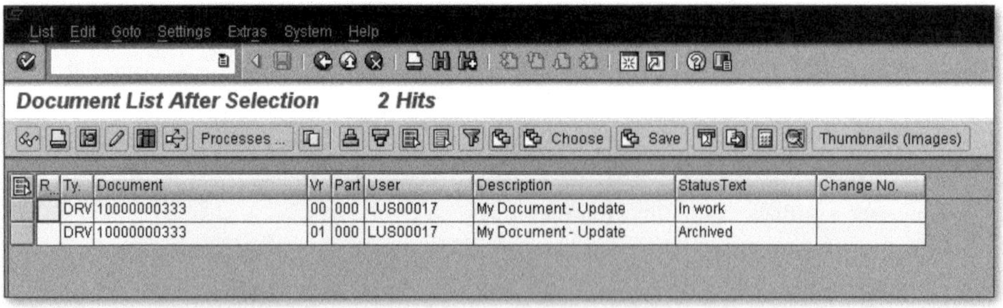

Figure 3.21 Search Results Returned for Document Search

3.5.2 Search for a Document Information Record using Document Type and Classification Attributes as the Criteria

Earlier in this chapter, you learned about attributes that are maintained on the ADDTNL DATA tab, and their importance. Through demonstration you will now gain an understanding of the benefit of these attributes. You will understand that defining and spending time figuring out which attributes should be associated with a document information record will pay off by decreasing the time users will spend searching.

For the example, you will be using document type "DRW." This document type has a default class associated with it, which in turn has the following attributes or characteristics associated with it:

▶ FORM SIZE

▶ DATA CARRIER

▶ LINE NUMBER

For search criteria, enter the value "DRW" in the DOCUMENT TYPE field and then select the CLASSIFICATION (*) tab. As shown in Figure 3.22, enter values for FORM SIZE and DATA CARRIER. Use the values you entered during the previous exercises. Click on the EXECUTE button to start the search. Document information records matching the search criteria will be returned.

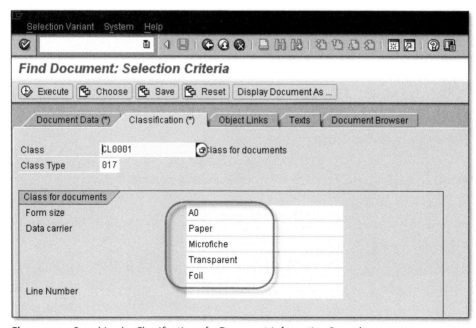

Figure 3.22 Searching by Classification of a Document Information Record

3.5.3   Search for a Document Information Record by Object Link

When you created document information records earlier in this chapter, you linked them to a material master. You will now learn that it is possible to find all document information records linked to a specific object. This is powerful because you can find all document information records related to a single or set of objects in one search.

Select the OBJECT LINKS (*) tab and then select the MATERIAL MASTER tab. As shown in Figure 3.23, enter the material master number to which you linked your document information record in the earlier exercises. Click on the EXECUTE button to start the search. Document information records matching the search criteria will be returned.

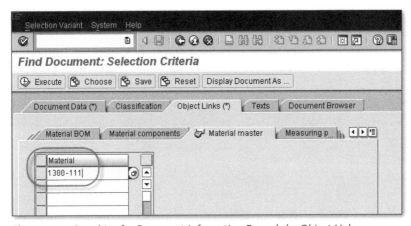

Figure 3.23   Searching for Document Information Records by Object Links

3.5.4   Search Long Text for a Document Information Record

You can search for document information records by long text. The long text is what is maintained beyond the short description. Instructions for maintaining long text were given earlier in this chapter.

To search for document information record by long text, select the tab TEXTS. As shown in Figure 3.24, under SEARCH TERM, enter a value to search for. You may use "*" as a wildcard character. You can also enter multiple values to search on, using the "and" and "or" operators.

After search criteria have been entered, click on the EXECUTE button to start the search. Document information records matching the search criteria will be returned.

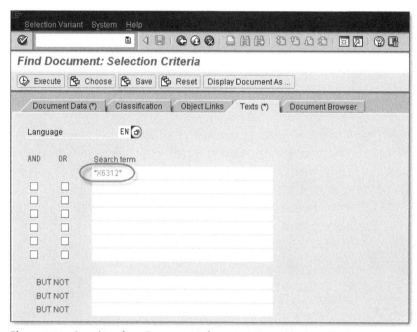

Figure 3.24 Searching for a Document Information Record by Long Text

3.5.5   Full Text Search

You can also do a full text search on the contents of original files that are stored in the system. The use of a full text search requires a content server to be set up and the settings for indexing to be complete. These topics are discussed in the chapter on the SAP DMS infrastructure, Chapter 5.

To execute a full text search, enter the term you want to search on in the SRCH TXT field. An example is shown in Figure 3.25. Click on the EXECUTE button to execute a full text search through the original files that have been indexed by the indexing process. After searching through the index, the document information records that have original files associated with the search term will be returned in the search list.

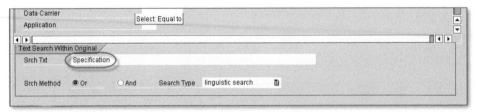

Figure 3.25 Searching for a Document Information Record using a Full Text Search

3.6 Additional SAP DMS Functionalities

So far in this chapter, you have learned the basics of creating, changing, displaying, and searching for document information records. Let's move on to additional functionalities that can be used during the creation, change, or display processes. These functions cover a wide variety of activities you'll need to complete while working with document information records. They include everything from copying an existing document information record to setting a revision level.

3.6.1 Copy a Document Information Record

When creating a document information record using Transaction CV01N, you can copy from an existing document information record by filling in the information in the template area. This includes the document number, part, and version you wish to copy from. All information from the template document information record will be copied to the new document information record.

3.6.2 Delete a Document Information Record

At times, you will want to delete a document information record from the system. This is accomplished by setting the deletion indicator on the document information record you want to delete. To do so, open the document information record in change mode and double-click on the selection box next to the field DELETION FLAG. As an alternative, you can follow the menu path DOCUMENT • CHANGE DELETION INDICATOR.

To actually delete of document information record, you need to execute the program "MCDOKDEL" using Transaction SE38.

3.6.3 Show the Sequence of Sources

You can find out whether a document information record was copied from another document information record by following the menu path EXTRAS • SEQUENCES OF SOURCES. The report will also give you the sources for those document information records.

3.6.4 Creating and Displaying the Document Hierarchy

You can create a hierarchy of document information records. This is accomplished by filling out the information in the SUPERIOR DOCUMENT area of the document information record. You identify a superior document by adding its document number, type, part, and version.

The hierarchy functionality is useful for relating document information records together. Through the hierarchy, you can identify one document record as part of a larger set of document information records.

To display the hierarchy, follow the menu path EXTRAS • HIERARCHY. The report will show the complete hierarchy.

3.6.5 Display the Status Log

Information is recorded at each status change of the document information record. You can review this information by following the menu path EXTRAS • STATUS LOG. Key information you will find includes a record of when the status changed, who changed it, a short description, and also whether any digital signatures were made.

3.6.6 Set and Display Revision Levels

You can assign a revision level to a document information record. To do so, you must have a change number associated to the document information record and one of the statuses in the status network must have the setting RELEASE FLAG checked. When this status is set, the system will prompt you and check whether you want to assign a revision level to the document information record.

A revision level is often used as an indicator of a major release. Document versions are usually used for minor releases. Users should take special note or action when using a document information record with a revision level.

3.6.7 Execute a Document Where Used

You can include a document information record in a BOM, or as part of a document structure. The "document where used" report will show you in which BOM or document structure the document information record is included. To execute this report, follow the menu path ENVIRONMENT • DOCUMENT WHERE USED.

3.6.8 Create a Document Structure

You can create a document structure or a document BOM. This functionality is used mostly when interfacing a CAD system that has an assembly structure, such as CATIA V5 or UG NX, to SAP DMS. This assembly structure will be maintained via a document structure. When working with a CAD system interfaced to SAP DMS, special functionality in the CAD Desktop (Transaction CDESK) is provided for managing document structures associated with the assembly structure of a CAD application.

To create a document structure, follow the menu path ENVIRONMENT • DOCUMENT STRUCTURE • CREATE. You will be taken to the initial screen for Transaction CV11 (Create Document Structure). Here you will verify that you want to create a document structure for the selected document information record. Press [Enter] and add the document information records to the table. This is very similar to building a regular material master-based BOM.

3.6.9 Copy an Original File to a Local Directory

At times, you will want to copy an original file associated with a document information record to your local machine. You can use this functionality when you are not checking out the file for change, but simply need a local copy. To do this, select the original file and follow the menu path ORIGINALS • COPY TO. After you select the file, you will be asked to identify where you would like to store it on your local machine.

3.6.10 Reset Check Out

If you have checked out an original file, you might at times want to cancel the check out. This could be, for example, because the locally checked out file has been corrupted and cannot be stored back into the system. To reset the check out, select the original file and follow the menu path ORIGINALS • RESET CHECK OUT. The padlock icon associated with the original file will close to indicate that the checkout has been cancelled.

3.7 Product Structure Browser

Earlier in this chapter you learned how to link a document information record to another SAP object, such as the material master. You will now learn about the SAP Product Structure Browser (Transaction CC04), which takes advantage of these object links.

The SAP Product Structure Browser is an excellent tool for consumers of information. A *consumer* is someone who searches for information; he does not create it. As an example, let's imagine you are a person on the manufacturing floor who needs access to all drawings for a product you are building, and for which you only know the material master number. In Transaction CC04, you can execute a search by the material master number and, as shown in Figure 3.26, the following information is returned:

- ▸ All documents linked to the material master
- ▸ The BOM associated with the material master
- ▸ A WHERE-USED LIST to identify in which assemblies this material master is used

Also shown in Figure 3.26 is the capability to directly view original files associated with document information records. In some cases, many documents information records will be linked to a material master. With this capability, you can quickly view the original files associated with multiple document information records.

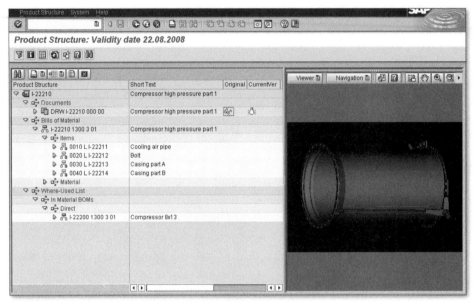

Figure 3.26 View of Results Returned in the SAP Product Structure Browser

Information returned is not limited to showing the relation between material master, BOM, and documents. As shown in Table 3.4, a lot of data can be returned if maintained, making the SAP Product Structure Browser a "one stop shopping" type of transaction for consumers of data.

Relations between SAP Objects Shown in the Product Structure		
Document	Document Revision	Change Number
Change Notification	Material	Material Revision
Material Specification	Equipment	Functional Location
Class	Characteristics	Configuration Definition
Configuration Folder	Baseline	BOM
BOM Item	Task List	Sequence
Operation	Material Inspection Characteristic	Distribution Order
Distribution Order Packages	Recipients	iPPE Nodes
Component Variant	iPPE Alternative	

Table 3.4 Relations shown in the SAP Product Structure Browser

3.7.1 Select the Focus of the SAP Product Structure Browser

In the SAP Product Structure Browser, you can select a variety of focuses to specify how you want to view information. As an example, if you select a focus of DOCUMENT, the report will be run with the document information record as the top information item and everything else displaying below it. As shown partially in Figure 3.27, focuses are selectable via correspondingly names tabs, including MATERIAL, DOCUMENT (Document information record), CHANGE NUMBER, CHAR. (Characteristic), CLASS, EQUIPMENT, FUNCTIONAL LOCATION, and CONFIGURATION DEFINITION.

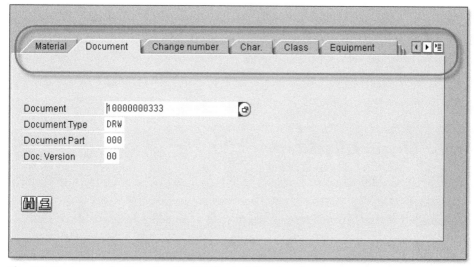

Figure 3.27 Focuses for Executing the SAP Product Structure Browser

To show you how it works, if you run a search with the document information record as the focus, the results returned will be similar to what is shown in Figure 3.28.

As demonstrated, the SAP Product Structure Browser is a powerful tool and can make finding information very easy. You will see through project experience that it is a tool users appreciate because of its ease of use and the amount of information displayed.

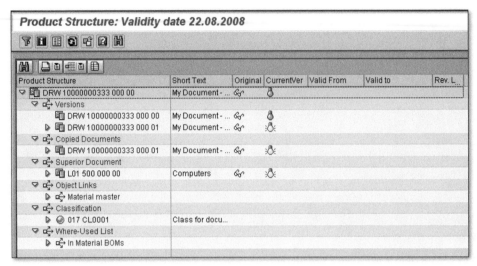

Figure 3.28 Results Returned in the SAP Product Structure Browser when Focusing on a Document Information Record

3.8 Classification Search

The attributes on the ADDNL DATA tab of a document information record are added through the use of a default class. The creation and change process of this class is managed through functionality provided by the SAP Classification system. In Chapter 4 on configuration, you will learn how to create a class. Right now, you will learn how to search using the classification search transaction CL30N (Find Objects in Classes). While the find Transaction CV04N (Find Document) offers similar functionality, it is important to gain some familiarity with the underlying technology that supports these attributes.

3.8.1 Example Classification Search

For the example classification search, you will search for document information records you created in the earlier exercises. This exercise assumes that you used document type DRW to create your example document information records.

To execute a classification search, open Transaction CL30N. As shown in Figure 3.29, enter a CLASS of "CL001" and a CLASS TYPE of "017". The class CL001 is the default class associated with document type DRW. The CLASS TYPE 017 is the class type that is associated with document information records. All classes you create for classifying document information records should belong to this class type. Press Enter .

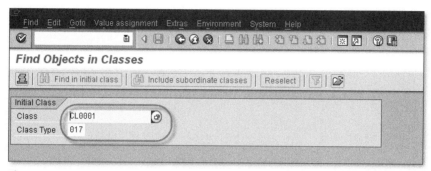

Figure 3.29 Entering the Class and Class Type on which to Search

On the next screen, you will see the characteristics associated with the class. Enter your search criteria in the characteristics on which you wish to search and click on the button FIND IN INITIAL CLASS. This executes the search. As shown in Figure 3.30, the search results are returned.

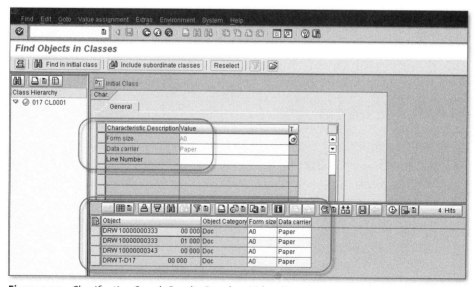

Figure 3.30 Classification Search Results Based on Values Input

In summary, the classification search capabilities are another tool you can use to search for documents.

3.9   Document Distribution

Through the document distribution function it is possible to distribute original files associated with a document information record. You can start a distribution through Transaction CVI8 (Start Document Distribution) or directly from the search results of Transaction CV04N (Find Document). This functionality is best demonstrated through Transaction CV04N because you will often want to distribute originals associated with a set of document information records. As an example, you might want to distribute all original files associated with document information records that are linked to a certain material or engineering change.

To start a distribution through Transaction CV04N, first enter your search criteria and execute. As shown in Figure 3.31, select the document information record you want to distribute, and then select the menu item EXTRAS • START DISTRIBUTION.

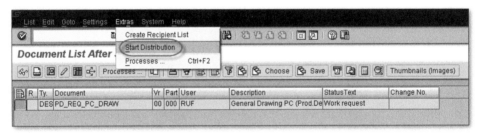

Figure 3.31 Start Document Distribution

As shown in Figure 3.32, create a recipient list on the START DISTRIBUTION screen. This can consist of internal users or external email addresses. If you want, you can keep the DISTRIBUTE IMMED. checkbox selected. If so, the distribution of the original file will start immediately on execution of the distribution.

On execution of the distribution, the original files are collected together and sent in an email to the users specified in the recipient list. The distribution order is also assigned a number and history or reporting on distributions is possible through Transaction CVI9 (Distribution Log).

This is the simplest type of distribution order. It is possible to have other types of distributions, such as sending via fax or copying original files to an external server.

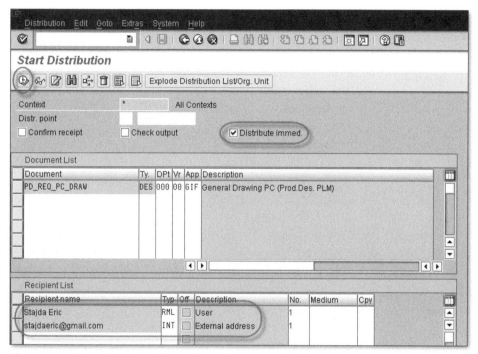

Figure 3.32 Enter a Recipient List and Start a Document Distribution

3.10 Internal Viewer

SAP provides you with an internal viewer to view graphic and other types of files. Use of the internal viewer saves the user from launching into a separate viewing application when displaying original files, thus providing a better user experience.

As shown in Table 3.5, a number of 2D and 3D formats are supported.

Format	Description
2D vector images files	AutoCAD DWG 2.5-14 (DWG)
	AutoCAD DXF R11-14 (DXF)
	AutoCAD DWF (DWF)
	CGM (CGM)
	IGES (IGES, IGS)
	HPGL/HPGL-2 (HPG, HPGL)
	HP ME 10/30 MI (MI)
	Calcomp (906, 907)
	CALS MIL-R Type I and Type II (MLR, MIL, MILR)
2D raster image files	Tagged Image File Format — monochrome, color, & grayscale (TIF)
	Windows Bitmap (BMP)
	JFIF Compliant (JPG, JPEG)
	Portable Network Graphics (PNG)
	EDMICS C4 (C4)
	(TLC)
	CompuServe (GIF)
	MIL-RII - TRIFF (FSX)
	SunRaster (RAS)
	PICT-Macintosh Paint (PCT, PICT)
	PC Paint (PCX)
	Microstation (DGN)
2D ASCII and Postscript files	ASCII Text (TXT)
	PostScriptl, II (PS)
	Encapsulated Postscript (EPS)
3D Models	*.JT - Direct Model
	*.WRL - Virtual Reality Modeling Language
	*.STL - Stereolithography

Table 3.5 Formats Supported by Internal Viewer

When you set up application types during the configuration process, you decide if the internal viewer will be used for a specific file type. This setup is covered in Chapter 4 on configuration.

As shown in Figure 3.33, when displaying an original file the file will show in the internal viewer if it is configured to do so.

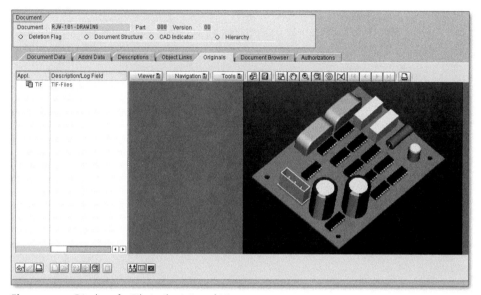

Figure 3.33 Display of a File in the Internal Viewer

Beyond viewing files, the internal viewer offers a number of additional tools, including:

- Navigation options including zoom, zoom area, center, and align
- Redlining of images
- Measurement tools
- Comparison of layers
- Printing directly from the viewer

One of the most useful tools from this list is the redlining tool. This allows users to make annotations or markups on a graphic image, which is often helpful in communicating changes that are required during an update or review process.

3.11 Summary

In this chapter, we have covered how to execute SAP DMS transactions, including the transactions to create, change, and display document information records. We also covered the Find Document transaction, which includes multiple methods for searching for documents, including searching by linked objects and full text searching. Beyond the basic operations, we covered functionalities such as how to copy a document information record and how to execute a document where used. These functionalities are important as you begin to grow your knowledge and become more advanced in your use of SAP DMS. We also looked at two additional transactions, the SAP Product Structure Browser and the Find Objects in Classes transaction.

It is important that you spend some time executing the transactions in this chapter before proceeding with the configuration of the system. In the next chapter, Chapter 4, you will learn how to configure SAP DMS.

In this chapter, you'll learn the basic SAP DMS configuration, and the complete information on the concepts and steps necessary to configure number ranges, document types, lab offices, and several other configuration items.

4 Configuring SAP DMS

In this chapter you will learn how to configure SAP DMS. We will discuss the configuration items most relevant to helping your project succeed. After they have been completed, you will be able to fully utilize SAP DMS. This includes creating document information records using your own document types and creating your own searchable attributes. All other items in this book build on the information presented in this chapter, including setting up security profiles and possibly developing workflows that can be started for specific document types and statuses.

4.1 Questions to Answer before Starting the Configuration

Make sure that you have spent a significant amount of time answering the questions presented in Chapter 2 (*Questions to Answer before Starting Your DMS Project*) before starting with the configuration of SAP DMS. You will need to take the answers to those questions and turn them into configuration values. As an example, in Chapter 2 you were asked to define which documents you want to manage with SAP DMS. Based on the answer to this question, you must now think about what document types you will create, what the status network will be for the document type, and what attributes will be associated.

In this chapter, we will provide you with an explanation for each configuration item, and — when available — best practices for completing the configuration.

4.2 SAP DMS Configuration in the SAP IMG

The entire SAP DMS configuration is completed by configuring settings in the SAP IMG (Transaction SPRO), following the path SAP CUSTOMIZING IMPLEMENTATION GUIDE • CROSS APPLICATION FUNCTIONS • DOCUMENT MANAGEMENT.

Under this IMG path you can configure settings for generating new document types, defining number ranges, setting up lab offices, defining revision levels, and a variety of other options.

4.3 Configuration Steps

Completing the SAP DMS configuration follows a set of individual configuration steps that have a logical flow. This flow takes into consideration dependencies between configuration activities and you are best-served following it when going through the configuration for the first time. Later, you can use this section as reference when making adjustments to your configuration.

4.4 Defining Number Ranges

The first step in the configuration is defining number ranges to be used for document information records. When you create a document information record, it is assigned a number. You will now decide what numbers and ranges of numbers are allowed. This is the first configuration step because during the next step — defining document types — you will use these number ranges.

To define number ranges, follow the IMG path DOCUMENT MANAGEMENT • CONTROL DATA • DEFINE NUMBER RANGE FOR DOCUMENT NUMBERS.

As shown in Figure 4.1, SAP has provided you with a base set of number ranges to work with. There are two types of number ranges, internal and external. An *internal* number range is used by the SAP system for assigning document information record numbers. An *external* number range is a range of numbers that will be available for users to assign document information record numbers to document information records. You can identify external number ranges by the checkmark in the EXT checkbox.

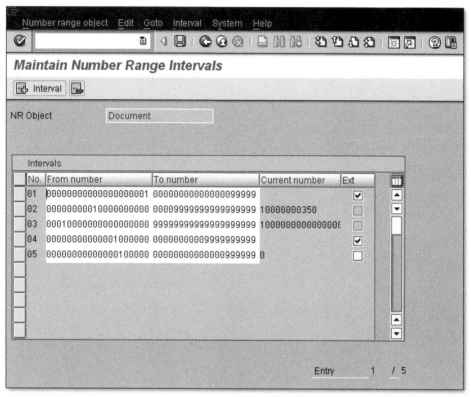

Figure 4.1 Internal and External Document Number Ranges, Delivered by SAP

If the out-of-the-box number ranges meet your number range requirements, further configuration is not required.

New number ranges are often defined so that a document information record can receive a shorter number. If you use the SAP-delivered document number ranges, your document information records for document types using internally assigned numbers will receive a number like "10000000240". This is typically not welcomed by users because of the length of the number. Depending on the number of document information records being stored in the system, you might consider a number range of 1000000-9999999. This is much shorter and enables you to store millions of documents using internal number assignment.

If you require a new number range, click on the INTERVAL button. A popup screen appears where you can enter a new number range. You will need to enter the following information:

▶ A number identifying the number range

▶ A FROM value

▶ A TO value

▶ Whether the number range should be used for external assignment

When defining new intervals you must avoid that they overlap with currently defined number ranges. If necessary, adjust the current FROM NUMBER and TO NUMBER values to not interfere with your new range.

Number ranges can also be deleted by selecting a range and clicking on the "-" (Delete Interval) button.

4.5   Creating Document Types

The most important configuration item is setting up the document types that will be used. To users, the document type is a highly visible element, and is the first thing they select when creating a document information record. The document type also has a lot of functionality attached to it, including:

▶ Status networks

▶ Additional attributes used for searching

▶ Rules around object linking

▶ Conversion processes for creating neutral files

▶ Security rules

Much thought needs be given to defining what document types you need. In Chapter 2, we talked about defining the documents you need to manage with SAP DMS. It is now time to turn the answer to that question into document types. Let's work with an example scenario in which you have chosen to manage the key engineering documents. They fall into the following categories:

▶ Specifications

▶ Test reports

▸ CAD drawings

▸ Customer requirements

You could now simply create a new document type for each of these categories. But before you do this, try to answer the following questions for each category. Based on how you answer the questions of status network, searching, object links, security, etc. – you will have different document types. This helps you define what document types you'll require.

▸ What is the status network?

▸ How do you want to search?

▸ What objects should you be able to link to?

▸ Are there different security requirements?

You might find that for the document category "specifications," you want to search by specification type. This would be an additional attribute on this document type. Searching by specification type would not, however, be relevant to the document category "test reports." For test reports, you might have a different set of attributes that are needed for searching. Based on different requirements, such as additional attributes, you will have different document types. You may also have different security requirements that specify that only a certain group of individuals can see documents that are in the category of "customer requirements." In addition, you might also want to control that customer requirements can only be linked to a customer object in SAP. This would not be the case for CAD drawings; they are only linked to the material master object.

In general, best practice is to keep the number of document types you create to a manageable number. It is easy to create a lot of document types. However, when this occurs, the list of document types from which users can choose becomes very long and possibly confusing.

For example, let's assume that the categories "specifications" and "test reports" have a lot in common. This means that they have the same search attributes, status work, security requirements, and object links. Therefore, you can create a document type of "ZSR" (Eng. Specs/Reports) for both categories. The other two categories do not have much or anything in common; therefore you can create two separate document types "ZCD" (CAD Drawings) and "ZCR" (Customer Requirements) for the two categories.

4.5.1 Configuration Location

To create document types, follow the IMG path DOCUMENT MANAGEMENT • CONTROL DATA • DEFINE DOCUMENT TYPES.

4.5.2 Configuration Example

You will now configure the system based on the example category "specifications," discussed previously. You will create a document type of "ZSR" with a description of "Eng. Specs/Reports." This document type will have a very simple status network, and it will only be able to be linked to a material master. You will also define three additional attributes for the document type: the specification/report type, the associated project, and a characteristic indicating whether the document is a controlled document requiring approval for release.

4.5.3 Configuration Steps

The document type configuration consists of the following four steps:

1. Create the initial document type.

2. Define the status network.

3. Define which object links are relevant for the document type.

4. Create a class using SAP Classification to support additional attributes.

Step 1 - Create the Initial Document Type

Select the configuration item DEFINE DOCUMENT TYPES to begin the configuration. On the first screen that appears, click on the NEW ENTRIES button. This will initiate the creation of the new document type. On the screen that appears, you will enter values and settings to define the document type. The available values and settings are defined in Table 4.1 and Table 4.2.

Table 4.1 shows document type attributes that define how the document type will function in the system. For each attribute, a brief description, as well as a value for our example scenario, is provided.

Attributes Area		
Field	**Description**	**Value**
Document Type	A high level classification that categorizes documents.	ZSR
Doc. Type Desc.	The document type description.	Eng. Specs/ Reports
Use KPro	Identifies whether original files will be checked into a KPro Content Server.	Checked
Status Change	Specifies whether the status of the document information record must be changed when a field is updated.	Unchecked
Rev. Lev. Assgmt	Indicates whether revision levels can be assigned to a document information record when associating a change master.	Checked
Version Assgmt	Controls automatic version assignment.	Checked
Archiving Authorization	Specifies whether original files associated with a document information record can be archived.	Unchecked
Change Docs	Indicates whether change documents should be created when a document information record is changed.	Checked
CM Relevnce	Determines whether the document type is controlled by configuration management.	Unchecked
Number Assgmt	Controls what type of number assignment will be allowed for the document type.	1
Internal Number Range	Specifies which number range will be used for internal assignment.	02
External Number Range	Specifies which number range will be used for external assignment.	Blank
Number Exit	Specifies the program that controls number assignment and versioning for document information records. The default is MCDOKZNR.	MCDOKZNR
Vers. No. Incr.	Identifies which increment will be used for version assignment.	1

Table 4.1 Attributes for the Document Type Configuration

Attributes Area		
Field	**Description**	**Value**
AlternativeScreen	The number of the screen that replaces the standard system screen for the document type (program SAPLCV110; screen 0102).	Blank
AScEx.	The name of the program in which form routines for the PBO and PAI time point of an alternative screen are stored.	Blank
File Size	The maximum original file size to be stored in the SAP database. This setting is only relevant when not using the KPro Content Server.	0
Class Type	The class type for the default class to be assigned to the document type. The typical setting is 017.	Blank
Class	The default class to be assigned to the document type. Fields in the class will display on the Additional data tab of the document information record.	Blank
Default Appl.	The default workstation application that is set when creating original files.	Blank
Dis. WS applic.	The application that is copied as the default value for the distribution.	Blank

Table 4.1 Attributes for the Document Type Configuration (Cont.)

In Table 4.2 you will find example values for the fields on the document information record. For each field, you can specify that it should be suppressed, for display only, an optional entry, or required.

This functionality is very useful when you want to suppress or hide fields that are not relevant to your business requirements. For example, if you do not intend to use engineering change management on document information records, you can suppress the field CHANGE NUMBER. This will make it invisible to users. As mentioned, you can also make certain fields required, such as adding a description to the document information record. Suppressed fields are indicated by a "-" symbol and required fields by a "+" symbol.

Field Selection Area	
Field	**Value**
Class Data	Blank
Hierarchy Indicator	-
Document Status	Blank
Document Description	+
User	Blank
Authorization Group	Blank
Lab/Office	+
Change Number	Blank
CAD Indicator	-
Superior Document	-
WS Application 1	Blank
WS Application 2	Blank
CM Relevance	-

Table 4.2   Field Selection for the Document Type Configuration

Given the settings in Table 4.2, the fields DOCUMENT DESCRIPTION and LAB/OFFICE will be required entries. The fields HIERARCHY INDICATOR, CAD INDICATOR, SUPERIOR DOCUMENT, and CM RELEVANCE will be suppressed or hidden.

After all values have been entered, the configuration of your document type ZSR should look as the one shown in Figure 4.2. You can save your work by clicking on the Save icon. It is a good idea to do this now, before moving on to the next step.

Step 2 – Define the Status Network

The next step is defining the status network for the document type. As discussed earlier, you will define a simple status network for the new document type ZSR. Specifically, a document information record of document type ZSR will start with an initial status of "In Work" and will then be allowed to proceed to a status of "Request Approval." From "Request Approval," it can move back to "In Work" or to a status of "Completed." The status of "Completed" signifies that the document information record is released and you can assign a revision level if you desire.

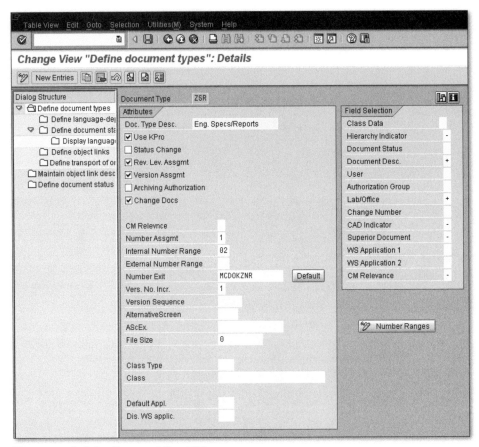

Figure 4.2 Defining Document Type ZSR

With the document type ZSR open, in the DIALOG STRUCTURE pane, select the configuration item DEFINE DOCUMENT STATUS. Select the button NEW ENTRIES, which initiates adding a status to the status network. On the next screen, enter the value "IW" (for In Work) in the field DOCUMENT STATUS. You can also use the dropdown list next to the field to select the value. Next, you need to start setting the attributes for the status, which are described in Table 4.3.

Attributes Area		
Attribute	**Description**	**Value**
Object Check	Confirms that the object link a user enters exists. For example, if a user attempts to link a document information record to a material master, the system will check to make sure the material master exists.	Checked
Release Flag	Indicates whether a version of a document information record is released. Controls assignment of revision level to the document information record.	Unchecked
Content version	Indicates whether a content version is created for an original file associated with a document information record each time it is stored.	Checked
Check in	Indicates whether files are automatically checked in when the status is set.	Unchecked
Complete for ECM	Shows that a document with this status is "completed" for engineering change management purposes.	Unchecked
Distr. lock	If set, document information records with this status are not distributed via ALE.	Unchecked
Check-In Required	Indicates whether all original files associated with the document information record must be checked in before the status can be set.	Unchecked
Fld sel.	Determines whether a status log entry is required, no entry, or optional.	"-" (No Entry)
Status type	Lets you select the status type. For our example scenario, you are selecting "I", which means that this will be the initial starting status for the document information record. Other status types are available, including temporary, locked, and archived. The locked status will be used later so that no further changes can be made to the document information record.	"I" (Initial)

Table 4.3 Attribute Settings for Status In Work

Attributes Area		
Attribute	**Description**	**Value**
Prev. 1 - 6	These fields are where you build the status network. In this case, you will set the status of "RA" as a previous status. This indicates that you can move back to the "In Work" status from "Request Approval." (When we get to defining the next status of "Request Approval," the "In Work" status will be the previous status for "Request Approval."	"RA" (Request Approval)
Workflow Task: "Object Type" and "Object ID"	The workflow definition that is triggered when the status is set.	Blank
Program exit	The custom program that is executed when the status is set.	Blank
Form routine	The sub-program to be executed from a program as soon as a document info record with this status is saved.	Blank
SignStrat.	The digital signature strategy that is executed when the status is set.	Blank

Table 4.3 Attribute Settings for Status In Work (Cont.)

When you're done, your ATTRIBUTES settings for the status IN WORK should now look as they do in Figure 4.3. Click on the Save button to save your entries.

The next step is creating the additional statuses of "Request Approval" and "Completed." Click on the NEXT STATUS button and use the blank entry screen that displays to begin working.

Defining the Request Approval Status

The "Request Approval" status will follow the "In Work" status. It signals that you are requesting document approval. During approval, the document should be locked for changes.

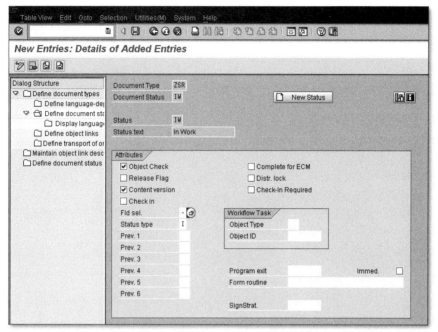

Figure 4.3 Definition of Status in Work

The settings for the "Request Approval" status are outlined in Table 4.4.

Attribute	Value
Document Status	RA
Object Check	Checked
Check In	Checked
Fld sel.	"-" (No Entry)
Status type	"S" (Locked)
Prev. 1	"IW" (In Work)

Table 4.4 Attribute Settings for Status Request Approval

The key setting to take into consideration here is the setting PREV. 1. By setting it to "IW" (In Work), you are indicating that you move from the status of "In Work" to "Request Approval."

When entries are complete, save your settings and continue with defining the next status.

Defining the Completed Status

The status "Completed" should follow the status "Request Approval" and it will be the final status in the status network. This status will signify that when set, the document information is complete and released. No updates to the document information record are allowed after this status is set.

The settings for the "Request Approval" status are outlined in Table 4.5.

Attribute	Value
Document Status	CP
Object Check	Checked
Check In Required	Checked
Complete for ECM	Checked
Release Flag	Checked
Fld sel.	"-" (No Entry)
Status type	"S" (Locked)
Prev. 1	"RA" (Request Approval)

Table 4.5 Attribute Settings for Status Completed

After your entries are complete, click on the Save icon. This completes building the status network. The configuration of your status network should now look as shown in Figure 4.4.

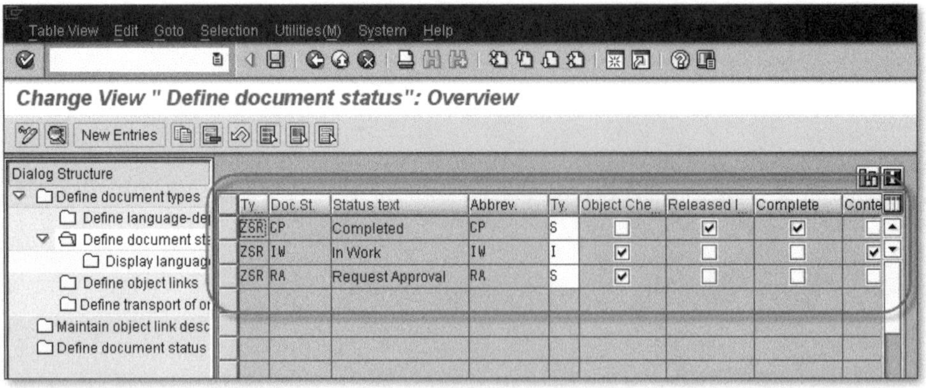

Figure 4.4 Completed Status Network Configuration

If you create a document information record using document type ZSR, the status network graphic will look like the one shown in Figure 4.5. You can review the status network from the document information record under the menu path EXTRAS • STATUS NETWORK.

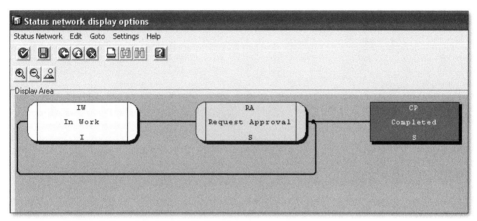

Figure 4.5 View of Completed Status Network

Step 3 – Define Object Links

As shown in Table 4.6, a great number of SAP objects exist to which you can link document information records. Object links are powerful because they make document information records visible in many different transactions across the SAP system.

Objects		
Engin. Change Mgmt	Functional Location	Case
Asset master record	Appropriation req.	Quality Notification
Claim	Measuring Points	Organizational Unit
Prod.resources/tools	Object Link	Patient
cProjects Elements	Ref. location	Packing Instruction
Document Info Record	Class	Maintenance notific.
Purchase Req. Item	Customer	PPE Node
Purchase Order Item	Vendor	Production Order

Table 4.6 Possible Object Links for a Document Information Record

Objects		
Equipment Master	Material Master	PPE Variant
Subst.rep.gen.var.	Plant Material	WBS Element
Substance Master	Material Component	QM Info Record
Notification	Service Notification	Layout Area
Inspection Methods	BOM Header	Layout Module
QM Info Record: SD	Material BOM	Sales Document Item
Equip. Req. (RMS)	BOM Item	Baseline
Process (RMS)	SAP EIS: Master Data	Configuration Folder
Rental Unit	Room	WCD Item
Lease	Management Contract	Work Approval
Asset group	Network	Layout area item
Real Estate	Request	WCD Item
Buildings	Work Clearance Doc.	Work Approval

Table 4.6 Possible Object Links for a Document Information Record (Cont.)

As a simple example, you will configure the document type ZSR so that a document information record of this type can link to a material master.

With the document type ZSR open, in the DIALOG STRUCTURE pane, select the configuration item DEFINE OBJECT LINKS. Next, click on the button NEW ENTRIES.

As shown in Figure 4.6, enter "MARA" in the OBJECT field and save the change. This is the only configuration required to be able to link a document information record of type ZSR to a material master. If you want, you can add a few other objects to which you can link. Simply click on the NEXT ENTRY button and select a new object to link to.

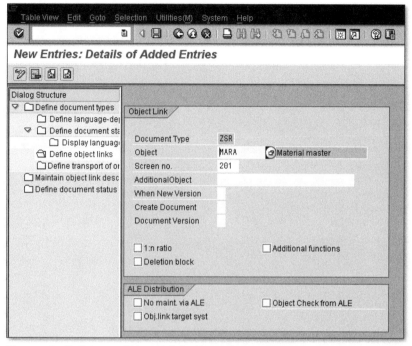

Figure 4.6 Defining an Object Link for Material Master

Step 4 – Create a Default Class for Additional Attributes

In the next step you will create a default class for the additional attributes on this document type. As mentioned earlier, the three additional attributes are specification/report type, associated project, and a characteristic indicating whether the document is a controlled document requiring approval for release.

The creation of the default class is completed via Transaction CL02 (Class Maintenance). As shown in Figure 4.7, on the initial screen of this transaction, enter a CLASS name of "ZSR_CLASS" and a CLASS TYPE of "017". Click on the CREATE button to begin entering the characteristics.

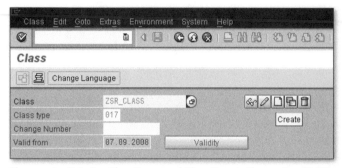

Figure 4.7 Entering Class Name and Class Type in Transaction CL02

On the next screen that appears, enter a class description of "Default Class for Document Type ZSR" in the BASIC DATA area. Next, select the tab CHAR. to start defining the characteristics. You will create three characteristics, as described in Table 4.7.

Characteristic	Description
ZSPECREPTYPE	Spec./Report Type
ZPROJECT	Project
ZCONTROLLED	Controlled Document

Table 4.7 Characteristics to Be Created

To create a characteristic, enter the name of the characteristic and press Enter. You will be prompted to confirm that you want to create the characteristic. Click on YES, and on the next screen, enter the DESCRIPTION of the characteristic and a DATA TYPE. Example settings for the characteristic ZSPECREPTYPE are shown in Figure 4.8.

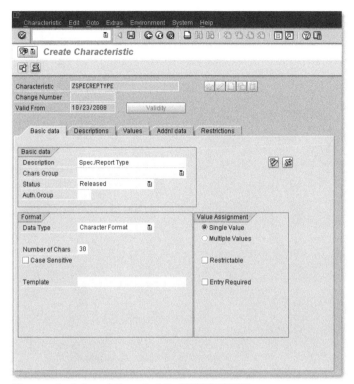

Figure 4.8 Setup of Characteristic ZSPECREPTYPE

Next, you will define a set of values for the characteristic, to provide users with values from which to pick. Example values are shown in Figure 4.9.

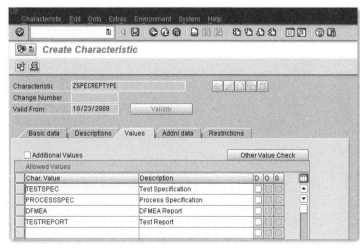

Figure 4.9 Creating Values for Characteristic ZSPECREPTYPE

After entering values, click on the Save button. You are returned to the main screen for adding characteristics to the class. Follow the procedure you used to create the characteristic ZSPECREPTYPE to create the characteristics ZPROJECT and ZCON-TROLLED. If you want, you can vary the values allowed for each characteristic. When completed, the screen where you add characteristics to the class should look similar to the one shown in Figure 4.10. Click on the Save button to save the class.

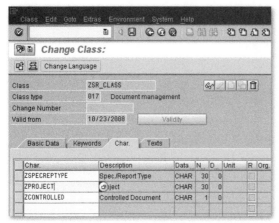

Figure 4.10   The Change Class Screen after Adding Several Characteristics Completed

The last step in this process is adding the new class as the default class for the document type ZSR. In the IMG, under the document management configuration, open the document type configuration for document type ZSR. In field CLASS TYPE enter "017" and in the field CLASS enter "ZSR_CLASS." This will associate it as the default class. The results of associating this class as the default class are shown in Figure 4.11. The characteristics in the class are available for users to fill out. More important, they are also available to search on.

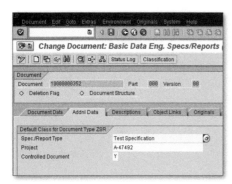

Figure 4.11   Results of Adding Class ZSR_CLASS to Document Type ZSR

4.6   Defining Laboratories/Design Offices

In this activity you will define the laboratories or design offices. This configuration is related to the field LAB/OFFICE on the document information record and populating the list of values available for selection by users.

> **Special Notice**
>
> This configuration also controls the configuration for the field LAB/OFFICE on the material master. This needs to be taken into consideration when updating the values.

The key thing to think about here is what you want the field LAB/OFFICE on the document information record and the material master to specify or mean. This field is often used to specify the design responsible location or group. If it is used to represent the design responsible location, the configuration will be populated with all of the engineering centers that exist in an organization. If it is meant to be the responsible group, it will be populated with a list of engineering groups that might be spread out across multiple locations. These are just a few possibilities of how this field can be used, but you need to be clear as to what the field means in your company before proceeding with the configuration.

The definition of laboratories or design offices is completed by following the IMG path DOCUMENT MANAGEMENT • GENERAL DATA • DEFINE LABORATORIES/DESIGN OFFICES.

As shown in Figure 4.12, this configuration activity is straightforward. You can add entries by clicking on the button NEW ENTRIES. You can delete entries by clicking on the "-" button. After updating the entries, click on the Save button.

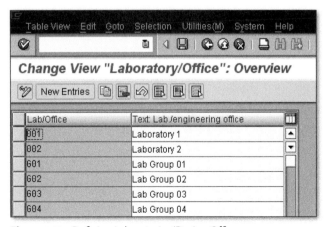

Figure 4.12   Defining Laboratories/Design Offices

4.7 Defining Revision Levels

You will now define revision levels that can be assigned to a document information record. Revision levels are assigned to a document information record when using a change number and specifying a status in the status network that has the "Release Flag" set.

As mentioned previously, revision levels are often used as an indicator of a major release. Document versions, on the other hand, are used to indicate minor releases.

To define revision levels follow the IMG path DOCUMENT MANAGEMENT • CONTROL DATA • DEFINE REVISION LEVELS.

As shown in Figure 4.13, the configuration activity is straightforward. You add entries by clicking on the button NEW ENTRIES, and you delete entries by clicking on the "-" button. After updating the entries, click on the Save button.

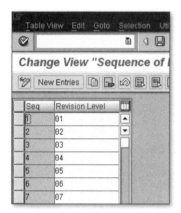

Figure 4.13 Defining Revision Levels

4.8 Defining Workstation Applications

When you store an original file on a document information record, you associate that file to a workstation application. The workstation application controls how original files are processed. More specifically, it controls what application is started when displaying or changing an original file, and how the original file is printed.

You will define a workstation application for each application file type you want to store in SAP DMS. For example, if you want to store files generated in the application Visio, you define a workstation application that is selected when someone checks in a Visio file. The selection of the workstation application is based on the extension of the Visio file, that is, the extension VSD. You can also specify that the Visio application launches whenever someone changes or displays a Visio file that is associated with a document information record.

4.8.1 Example Workstation Application – Microsoft Word

As an example configuration we will explore the settings for the workstation application "WRD," for Microsoft Word documents. You can then configure additional workstation applications required for your project. Beyond the workstation "WRD," SAP provides additional applications in the system from which you can learn.

4.8.2 Workstation Application Details

Execute the configuration item by following the IMG path DOCUMENT MANAGE-MENT • GENERAL DATA • DEFINE WORKSTATION APPLICATION.

On the first screen that appears, double-click on the workstation application WRD. As shown in Figure 4.14, this takes you to the DETAILS screen where settings are configured for the workstation application.

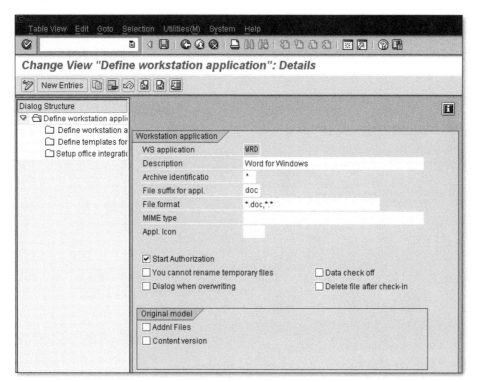

Figure 4.14 Details for Workstation Application WRD

Table 4.8 contains descriptions and sample values for each of the detailed settings for workstation application WRD.

Setting	Description	Value
WS application	The abbreviation for the workstation application.	WRD
Description	A short description of the workstation application.	Word for Windows
Archive Identification	The key used to uniquely identify the archive in which the original application files processed and archived with this application are stored.	* You can select any of the defined archives
File suffix for appl.	The suffix added to the original files when processing. This includes the change and display processes.	doc
File format	The file extensions that are relevant to the workstation application. The workstation application will be suggested when an original file with the extension is stored.	*.doc, *.*
MIME type	The HTML content type.	Blank
Appl. icon	The icon that will be displayed in the document information record next to the stored original file.	Blank
Start authorization	Indicates whether the application can be started.	Checked
You cannot rename temporary files	When displaying an original file, this indicator determines whether the file can be renamed.	Unchecked
Dialog when overwriting	If set, a warning dialog appears to confirm that you want to overwrite a file if it already exists on the local machine.	Unchecked
Data check off	Indicates whether the system checks for the existence of original files that are processed with this workstation application in the given path.	Unchecked

Table 4.8 Details of Workstation Application WRD

Setting	Description	Value
Delete file after check-in	Specifies whether files on the local machine are deleted after storage has occurred.	Unchecked
Addnl Files	If this indicator is set, you can store additional files associated to the original file with each original file. As a result, when checking out an original file, the additional files are included.	Unchecked
Content version	Indicates whether content versions are allowed for the workstation application. If set here and in the status network, a content version is created each time the original file is updated.	Unchecked

Table 4.8 Details of Workstation Application WRD (Cont.)

4.8.3 Define Workstation Application in Network

With the workstation application WRD selected, in the DIALOG STRUCTURE pane, open the configuration item DEFINE WORKSTATION APPLICATION IN NETWORK. During this step, you will define how the application launches when displaying or changing an original file associated to the workstation application. For each data carrier, you can have three application types or actions that can be configured:

▸ Display

▸ Change

▸ Print

This is illustrated in Figure 4.15.

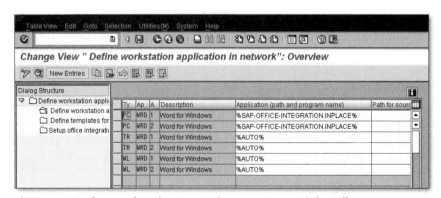

Figure 4.15 Definition of Workstation Applications in Network for Different Data Carriers

The key setting you need to be concerned with on the DETAILS screen for a specific data carrier and application type is the field PATH WITH PROG. NAME.

In most cases, you will use the value "%AUTO%" for this field. This allows Microsoft Windows to automatically locate the correct program when displaying or changing the original file. If required, you can also hardcode the path to the application that is launched.

Using Microsoft Office Integration

SAP provides integration to Microsoft Office products when viewing or changing these types of files. Therefore, if you use the value "%SAP-OFFICE-INTEGRATION. INPLACE%" in the field PATH WITH PROG. NAME, Microsoft Word will be opened directly in the SAP GUI when processing original files associated with this workstation application. Additional options are available when using this integration and are best explained through "F1" help.

Using the Integrated Viewer for Graphics Files

As mentioned previously in this book, SAP provides you with an integrated viewer for multiple graphic file types, including 2D and 3D formats. To use this viewer, you can fill in the value "EAIWeb.webviewer2D.1 %SAP-CONTROL%" in the field PATH WITH PROG. NAME. Additional options are available when using the integrated viewer and are best explained through "F1" help.

4.8.4 Define Templates for Original Files

You can define templates to use to generate new original files for a document information record. This is helpful when you want to use standard templates, such as report formats, for the generation of new original files. The definition of a template is shown in Figure 4.16. In this screen, you first specify the values for DOCUMENT TYPE, APPLIC. (application type), LANGUAGE, and NO (template number). These settings associate the template to the document type and workstation application. You then add a DESCRIPTION and either a SOURCE FILE or SOURCE DOCUMENT information record where the template can be found.

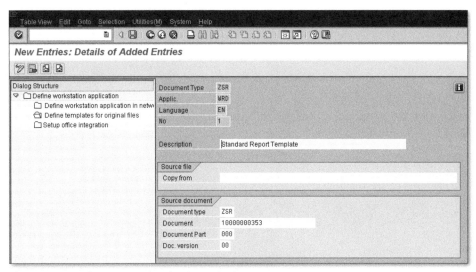

Figure 4.16 Defining a Template for Original Files

4.8.5 Set up Microsoft Office Integration

You can set up the Microsoft Office integration so that data from the document information record is passed to the Microsoft application. This is helpful when you want to use data from the document information record in the original file. This way, the original file can be dynamically updated based on attributes stored in the SAP system.

4.9 Maintain a Default Entry for Front End Type "PC"

To process original files correctly, you must maintain a default entry for the front end type "PC." This specifically allows PCs that do not have the variable "HOST-NAME" set to function properly.

To configure this setting, follow the IMG path DOCUMENT MANAGEMENT • GENERAL DATA • DEFINE DATA CARRIER.

In the configuration transaction, in the DIALOG STRUCTURE pane, select the item DEFINE DATA CARRIER TYPE "SERVER, FRONT END". From here, select the data carrier type PC and select IDENTIFY FRONTEND COMPUTERS, as shown in Figure 4.17. When you are on the appropriate screen, click on the button DEFAULT ENTRY. This will create an entry in the table with data carrier DEFAULT. This is all that needs to be done. The processing of original file should now function properly.

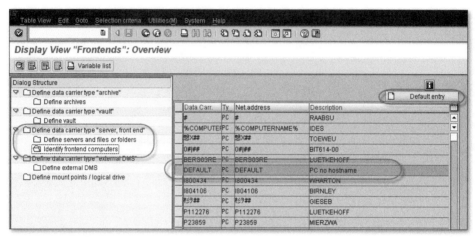

Figure 4.17 Define Default Entry for Data Carrier Type PC

4.10   Start Processing for Documents

During this next configuration step, you will add the capability to process a set of document information records that were returned from a search using the Find Document transaction, CV04N. Specifically, you will add the capability to set the deletion indicator for a set of selected documents.

Processing of documents is carried out by selecting a group of document information records in the search results and clicking on the PROCESSES ... button. As shown in Figure 4.18, you are then presented with a list of functions from which you can choose, to perform certain actions on the selected document information records. In this exercise, you will configure the system to set up the process to set the deletion flag across multiple document information records. However, this is just one example. Using ABAP, you can develop further functions to act upon document information records in specific ways. For example, you might create a function that selects a group of document information records and that then executes a process that downloads all of the original files to a specific location on the user's local machine.

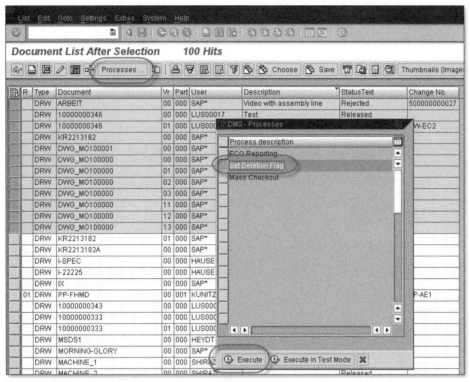

Figure 4.18 Processing the Selected Set of Document Information Records

To define processes, follow the IMG path DOCUMENT MANAGEMENT • GENERAL DATA • START PROCESSING FOR DOCUMENTS.

As mentioned previously, you will add a process for setting the deletion flag. Table 4.9 specifies the fields and values you will use to create a new entry. Figure 4.19 shows the DETAILS screen with the fields filled out.

Field	Value
Process cat.	All
Description	Set Deletion Flag
Sequence	1
Function Module	DMS_PROC_DOC_DELETE

Table 4.9 Fields and Values to Create a Process

The key setting here is FUNCTION MODULE. SAP has provided the function module DMS_PROC_DOC_DELETE, which carries out setting the deletion indicator, as an example on which you can build.

With this process, you are only setting the deletion indicator on the selected document information records. To delete them from the system, you need to run report MCDOKDEL in Transaction SE38.

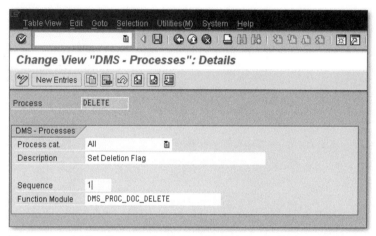

Figure 4.19 Adding Processes for Setting the Deletion Indicator

4.11 Define Workstation Application for Thumbnails

For each document type, you can define a workstation application containing a thumbnail image that will be displayed in the document information record. This capability is shown in Figure 4.20. The thumbnail is displayed because an original file with application type GIF is associated to the document information record. This functionality is helpful because users get a quick view of the original file attached to the document information record.

Added Value

If thumbnail applications are maintained, new functionality in the Find Document Transaction CV04N, allows you to display these thumbnail images in a grid instead of a table list of document information records. Users can then search through a returned set of document information quickly by looking at the thumbnail images.

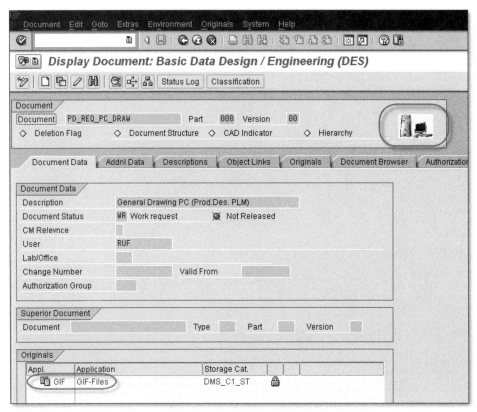

Figure 4.20 Displaying a Thumbnail in a Document Information Record

Defining workstation applications for thumbnails is performed by following the IMG path DOCUMENT MANAGEMENT • GENERAL DATA • SET UP WORKSTATION APPLICATION FOR THUMBNAILS (IMAGES).

To add a workstation application to be displayed as a thumbnail for a document type, click on the NEW ENTRIES button. Add the values for the fields DOCUMENT TYPE and APPLIC. (application) that you would like to use. Use only graphical applications such as applications that produce files with the GIF or JPG extension. Your entries should look as shown in Figure 4.21. When your settings are complete, click on the Save button.

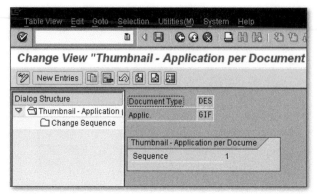

Figure 4.21 Adding an Application for Thumbnail Display

4.12 Define Profile

You can create profiles that set default values and settings for processing of original application files associated with a document information record.

For each profile, you can configure the following:

▶ Specific users or roles that are assigned to the profile.

▶ Workstation applications that will start when displaying or printing original files. Also, for each application you can configure the working directory to which you want to copy original files and a default storage category.

▶ A set of processes users can execute.

Using profiles is often helpful when you want to set up default applications and a default storage category for a set of users. For example, imagine that you have different applications and storage categories that users work with, based on their geographic location. Using profiles, you can set up defaults so that users do not need to make decisions about which applications or storage category to use.

You define profiles by following the IMG path DOCUMENT MANAGEMENT • GENERAL DATA • DEFINE PROFILE.

The first step is creating a new profile key. Click on the NEW ENTRIES button and enter a key and short description. Next, identify the users or roles to associate with this profile. This is accomplished by selecting the PROFILE KEY in the right pane, and then selecting the configuration item ASSIGN GROUPS/USER TO THE PROFILES in the DIALOG STRUCTURE pane, as shown in Figure 4.22.

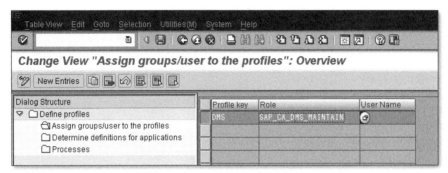

Figure 4.22 Assignment of Roles or Users to Profile

Next, select DETERMINE DEFINITIONS FOR APPLICATIONS in the DIALOG STRUCTURE pane. You will set up default applications for printing and display. You can also configure a default working directory and storage category for each application. Example settings are shown in Figure 4.23.

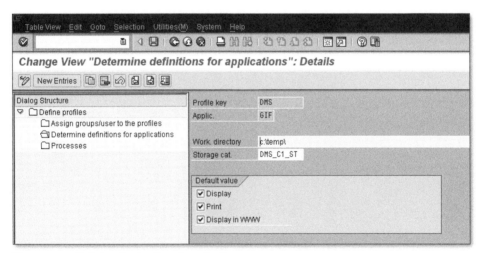

Figure 4.23 Defining Applications for a Profile

The last step is to define which processes are available to users. To add a process, select the configuration item PROCESSES in the DIALOG STRUCTURE pane, and add the processes you want to be available for the profile.

4.13   Additional Configuration Items

Additional configuration items are covered in their respective chapters. Specifically, Chapter 7 covers frontends to DMS, and explains how to configure Web documents. Also, the configuration of items such as the content server and how to set up a conversion process are discussed in Chapter 5.

4.14   Summary

In this chapter, we covered basic SAP DMS configuration. You should now know the concepts and steps necessary to configure number ranges, document types, lab offices, and several other configuration items. With the configuration complete, you have a baseline SAP DMS system in place that you can use. In terms of an actual SAP DMS implementation project, you might want to revisit the SAP DMS configuration topic throughout the life of the project. You can also start thinking about advanced topics, such as locking different frontends to SAP DMS, or enhancing the system using BAdIs and users exits.

In the next chapter, Chapter 5, you will learn about SAP DMS infrastructure requirements, and options for architecting an infrastructure solution.

This reviews the different infrastructure components that can be deployed during an SAP DMS implementation, including content servers, cache servers, index/TREX servers, and conversion servers.

5   Infrastructure Requirements

In this chapter you will learn about the four infrastructure components that are part of an SAP DMS implementation:

- Content server
- Cache server
- Index server (TREX)
- Conversion server

This chapter is structured to provide you first with a general overview of each infrastructure component and to then look at the different ways to combine the infrastructure components to architect a solution. For example, a simple architecture might have one content server and one index server to allow full text search capability. A more complex architecture might include multiple content, cache, and index servers. The architecture you end up with depends greatly on the environment in which you are implementing SAP DMS.

5.1   Content Server

The *content server* stores all of the original files that are associated with document information records in SAP DMS. When you check in an original file on a document information record, the file is taken from your local machine and stored on the content server.

The following facts about the content server are important to know:

▶ It is a separate server with its own installation of software.

▶ It can be installed on a Windows or UNIX based system (AIX, HP-UX, HP-UX, Linux, and Solaris).

▶ The server size is based on a variety of factors, including the number of users who access the server, and the number and type of documents being stored (e.g., CAD or Microsoft Office documents).

▶ Based on your environment's requirements, you can have one or many content servers.

▶ The underlying database can support up to 32TB of data.

▶ Installation of the content server software is a straight forward process.

▶ Some versions of the content server store original files in the file system, and not in the database.

Working Without a Content Server

If you do not set up a content server, you can store originals files in the main SAP database. This happens when you select storage category "DMS_C1_ST" when checking in an original file. Use of the SAP database for storing files is recommended only for a small number of original files. Storing large numbers of originals in the SAP database can cause issues with system performance.

5.1.1 Content Server Requests

When a user makes a request to process an original file, it goes first to the SAP system which identifies the content server where the original file is stored. From there, the information is sent back to the client. The client, in turn, makes a request to the content server. All requests and processing of original files is handled via HTTP; therefore a web server is set up on the content server. The web server has a service that talks to an instance of MAXDB. This instance of MAXDB keeps track of all original files that are stored. Storage of original files can be either in the MAXDB instance, or in the file system. Either way there will be an instance of MAXDB that knows where the files that need to be processed are located. If a request has been made to process an original file, the service on the content server will locate the original file and send it back to the client. This process is completely transparent to the user.

5.1.2   Key Transactions for the Content Server

Table 5.1 lists key SAP transactions related to the content server. Knowledge about these transactions will make setting up the content server much easier.

Transaction	Description
CSADMIN	Content server administration
OAC0	Content repository administration
OACT	Storage category administration
SCMSMO	Monitoring for content and cache servers

Table 5.1   Key Content Server Transactions

5.1.3   Content Server Quick Installation Guide

After you have downloaded the content server software from the SAP Service Marketplace, only a handful of steps are needed for you to get the content server up and running:

1. Using the setup program, install the necessary content server software on the server.
2. In Transaction CSADMIN, link the SAP system to the content server.
3. In Transaction CSADMIN, create a repository on the content server.
4. In Transaction OAC0, link the repository to the SAP DMS.
5. In Transaction OACT, create storage categories in the repository.

You can then test the content server by storing an original file in the storage category you have configured.

5.2   Cache Server

A *cache server* is a separate server that usually resides at remote locations where no content server is installed. The goal of the cache server is to speed up access to original files for users in remote locations. The concept and use of a cache server is best explained through an example.

> **Example Cache Server Scenario**
>
> A company has an engineering facility in the United States and a manufacturing site in Romania. The engineering facility is the location where all of the documentation for producing the company's product is generated. Therefore, a content server is installed at this location. The users at the manufacturing facility access the data generated by engineering and a cache server is installed at this location. When a user at the manufacturing facility brings up a drawing of a product they produce for the first time, a copy of the drawing is pulled from the content server located at the engineering facility and placed into the cache server located at the manufacturing site. The next time a user from the manufacturing location brings up that same drawing, the system will first check to see if the most recent copy of the drawing is located on the cache server before attempting to pull it from the content server at the engineering facility.

There are a number of benefits to installing one or more cache servers. These include:

▶ Reducing access time to original files for remote users

▶ Reducing utilization of the wide area network

▶ Minimizing the required administration to maintain a cache server

If your project will have users from multiple, remote locations accessing documents stored in SAP DMS, you should consider having a cache server installed at those locations.

5.2.1 Key Transactions for the Content Server

Table 5.2 lists the key SAP transactions related to the cache server. Knowledge of these transactions is required to configure a cache server.

Transaction	Description
SCMSHO	Define the cache server by host name and location
SCMSCA	Define the cache server by host name, port, and appropriate HTTP script
SCMSIP	Locations of IP subnets

Table 5.2 Key Cache Server Transactions

5.2.2 Customizing for the Cache Server

The following Customizing settings need to be configured when setting up the cache server:

1. Define the caches in your system:

   ▶ Define the host name and locations (Transaction SCMSHO).

   ▶ Define the cache (Transaction SCMSCA).

2. Define locations for the following:

   Users (clients), using:

   ▶ Set/get parameter LCA.

   ▶ Host name (Transaction SCMSHO).

   ▶ Subnet (Transaction SCMSIP). SAP recommends that you use sub-nets when defining locations for users.

   The content server, using:

   ▶ Host name (Transaction SCMSHO). SAP recommends that you use host names when defining locations for Content Server.

   ▶ Subnet (Transaction SCMSIP).

You can then test the cache server by twice displaying a large original file that is stored on a remote content server. When the file is displayed the second time, access should be faster because the file is pulled from the local cache server rather than the remote content server.

5.3 Index Server (TREX)

The *index server*, or TREX, component lets you perform full text searches on original files that are stored on a content server. For the full text search to work, TREX makes a copy of the original files (Word, PDF, Text, etc.) located on the content server and temporarily stores them on the TREX server. An indexing process then creates a searchable index of the original files on this server. This process is similar in function to how Google and Yahoo, for example, create a searchable index of web pages. After the index is created, you can perform full text searches on the original files.

5.3.1 Benefits of Full Text Searching

The main benefit for full text searching is to provide users with another, powerful tool to search for document information records. Full text search capabilities go far beyond searching on attributes that are available on the document information record.

5.3.2 Executing a Full Text Search

As shown in Figure 5.1, full text searches are executed through Transaction CV04N (Find Document).

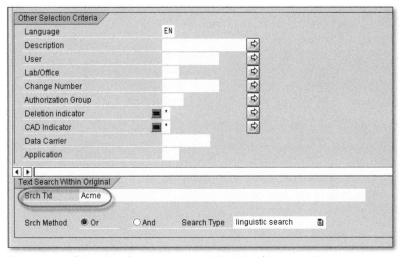

Figure 5.1 Full Text Search in Transaction CV04N (Find Document)

As mentioned previously, full text searching helps reduce the time users spend searching for documents. For your project, you will need to weigh whether this will be a beneficial component to configure.

5.4 Conversion Server

A *conversion server* is a server that carries out the process of converting original files on a document information record from one format to another. This conversion is triggered based on a status being set on the document information record.

Example Conversion Process

Let's look at an example where at the time a document information record reaches a status of "Released," the original files that are associated with the application type WRD (Microsoft Word) will be converted to PDF and attached to the document information record.

At the time of conversion, the Word files are transferred from the content server to the conversion server to be processed. When the conversion process is complete, the resulting file, in this case a PDF file, is returned to the content server and associated to the document information record.

Conversions of original files are often carried out for a variety of reasons. In the case of CAD files, the CAD data is converted to a neutral format because licenses for CAD applications are expensive and converting CAD files to a neutral file allows others to view the data without having to use a copy of the application. Another reason is the long term storage of documents. A PDF file is considered a long term storage format; therefore, it is good practice to convert many types of files to PDF so that they will still be viewable in the future, when the applications that generated the files are no longer supported.

5.4.1 SAP Software's Part in the Conversion Process

SAP provides the methodology to call a conversion process and to move the files back and forth from and to the content server. It does not provide the tools to perform the actual conversion on the server. For example, if you want to convert all of your CAD drawings to a neutral graphic file format such as TIF, you will need to write a script and provide the software that can carry out the conversion. This software and the necessary scripts would reside on the conversion server.

5.4.2 Sample Conversion Scripts and Tools

SAP provides example scripts and tools for starting a conversion. As stated in SAP Help, you will find the programs ConvUtil, ConvServSamp, and ConvRfc2Corba on the SAP server SapservX under the following path: *~ftp/general/misc/converter*.

5.4.3 Configuration of the Conversion Server

The configuration of a conversion server is completed by following the IMG path Document Management • Conversion of Original Application Files. Then, follow these three steps:

1. **Maintain the Converter:** Maintain the settings for the converter. This includes the converter destination, help program, and status.

2. **Define the conversion:** Defines when a conversion process is triggered and what original files should be converted.

3. **Maintain Location-Dependent Conversion Data:** Based on the storage category or content server, define which conversion process should be started.

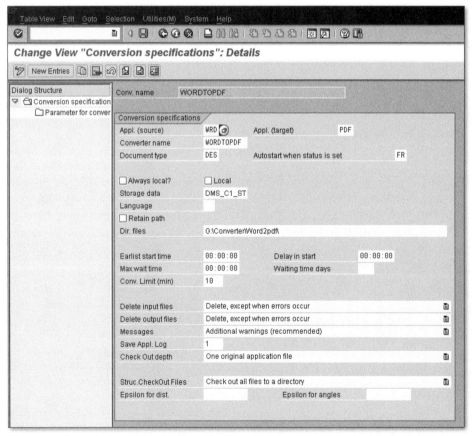

Figure 5.2 Example Conversion Configuration

Let's take a look at a few of the key settings in this definition.

First, let's look at the document type and the document status. You can see that the conversion process will start only for document type DES and when the status of the document information record is set to FR. When these conditions are met, the converter WORDTOPDF will be called. As defined in the fields APPL. (SOURCE) and APPL. (TARGET), the process will take original files of application type WRD and send them to the conversion server to be converted to type PDF.

A number of other settings can be configured for a conversion definition. This includes how to deal with input and output files, specifying the earliest start time for conversion, and specifying whether there should be a delay in starting the conversion.

5.5 Developing Your Infrastructure Architecture

You need to think about many factors when putting together your architecture, which can consist of one or more content, cache, TREX, or conversion servers. In general, what your architecture looks like depends on three elements:

- The types of users at each location
- The functionality you are implementing
- The wide area network's capabilities

5.5.1 Types of Users at Each Location

As mentioned briefly earlier in this book, two types of users exist: consumers and creators. To refresh your memory, consumers use the data others have generated. They display this information, but do not create new document information records. Creators, on the other hand, generate new original files and store them in the SAP DMS system.

For locations with a high number of creators, it is recommended that a content server is installed locally. This way, creators are not negatively impacted by (typically slow) wide area network speeds when checking in and checking out original files. Because creators are constantly working on original files, you want response times for them to be fast. Departments that typically have a significant number of creators are engineering departments because they are responsible for creating documents such as drawings, reports, and specifications.

If you have a location with a large number of consumers and only a small number of creators (if any), this location will only require a cache server.

5.5.2 Which Functionalities to Implement

Let's look at some considerations as to which functionalities you should implement. If you do not plan to convert original files to a neutral file format, you will not need a conversion server. If you do not plan to have full text search functionality, you will not need a TREX server. However, if you plan to have any of these functionalities, you will need to include them into your architecture. For conversion servers, you should plan to have one for each location at which you have a content server. This is especially true if you plan on performing conversions frequently because you do not want to pull original files across the wide area network for each conversion. You can also have multiple TREX servers; however, in most cases, a single TREX server will suffice. This server can index the contents of multiple content servers.

5.5.3 Wide Area Network Capability

If you have a wide area network, with excellent connectivity between all of the locations, it is possible to use a single content server. However, it is more likely that you have a wide area network with differing levels of service between different locations. If so, you will need to implement a solution that uses multiple content and cache servers.

Let's now look at three different architecture scenarios that vary in complexity. The first uses a single content server, the second uses a single local content server with a cache server for remote locations, and the last uses multiple content and cache servers.

Using a Single Content Server

The simplest architecture includes a single content server. This can be used to support creators and consumers at a small number of locations, or if the wide area network supports the complete enterprise with acceptable network performance. If you plan to implement a single content server, you will have to size your server appropriately for the amount of data and the number of users that will be accessing it.

Using a Single Local Content Server with a Cache Server for Remote Locations

The next level of architecture uses a single content server with cache servers at remote locations to support consumers and to help reduce access time for the remote users. The remote locations would still be able to check in original files to the content server; however, check-in times may not be optimal because of wide area network service levels between the remote locations and the content server.

Using Multiple Content and Cache Servers

If you must support multiple locations with consumers and creators at each location, you will likely need a solution with multiple content and cache servers. For each location with creators you will need a content server. These locations may also have a cache server because you will want to cache data coming from content servers located at other locations. You might also have sites with just a cache server, and no content servers.

As you can see, many possibilities exist when you combine the different infrastructure components. Which configuration you use, will depend on your requirements.

5.6   Summary

In this chapter, we've reviewed the different infrastructure components that can be deployed during an SAP DMS implementation. They include content servers, cache servers, index/TREX servers, and conversion servers. For each infrastructure component, you learned how it works and what its purpose is, along with the steps needed to configure the component in the system. Later, you learned different ways in which the components can be deployed, and what possible architectures can look like. With the information presented in this chapter, you can now start developing an architecture that will fit your environment.

In the next chapter, Chapter 6, we will cover the topic of setting up SAP DMS security.

This chapter reviews SAP DMS security and authorization concepts. Securing access to documents is a key component of every project.

6   SAP DMS Security

In this chapter, you will learn about SAP DMS security and how you can use it to control access to documents.

6.1   Defining Your Security Requirements

Before arriving at a discussion on the technical details of document security, it is important that you first define your document security requirements. The fundamental questions you need to answer are: *Who should have access to a document?* and *At what point(s) in time should access be granted?* Several factors will help determine the answers to these questions, including:

1. **Customer requirements:** If you are designing or building goods for a customer, does the customer require that you restrict access to documents that support the product?

2. **U.S. government requirements, specifically military requirements:** If you build products for the U.S. military, you must comply with ITAR requirements. That means that documents may only be shared with U.S. citizens, unless government approval is received or an exemption granted.

3. **Project security:** Should you only allow individuals involved in a project to access the related documents?

4. **Patent applications:** How do you manage access to documents that support a patent application? Should you restrict access until a certain point in the patent process is reached?

5. **Financial information:** Do documents contain financial information that if released could cause harm or hardship to the company?

6. **Flexibility:** How much effort are you willing to put into security management? Also, with each added layer of security, there is a cost for maintenance.

These are just a few points you need to take into consideration when defining your security requirements. You should make sure to give this topic plenty of thought.

6.2   Standard SAP DMS Authorization Objects

The SAP DMS system comes with a number of standard authorization objects that can be used to restrict user access to document information records, by the following key attributes:

- Authorization group
- Document type
- Document status

Beyond using the standard authorization objects, you can use two additional elements to restrict access. This includes the user of access control lists (ACLs), and custom authorization checks using the BAdI DOCUMENT_AUTH01. Both of these items are covered in later sections of this chapter.

It is important for you to understand that authorization objects are checked in a specific order to confirm that a user is allowed to open a document information record:

1. A check by the SAP system is made to make sure that the user has access to execute the transaction (e.g. Change Document – Transaction CV02N).
2. C_DRAW_BGR checks access based on the authorization group maintained in the document information record.
3. C_DRAW_TCD checks access based on document type and activity.
4. C_DRAW_TCS checks access based on document type, activity, and status.
5. An ACL check is performed.
6. A custom authorization check is performed.

It is important that you understand this order when setting up your security roles. It will make testing and verification of roles much simpler and clearer.

In the next sections of this chapter, you will learn about the standard SAP authorization objects. A description and example usage is provided for each object.

6.2.1 Authorization Object C_DRAW_TCD — Activities for Documents

Using authorization object C_DRAW_TCD, and based on a combination of activity and document type, you can control whether a user can process a document information record. Based on the document type, you may want to restrict what actions a user can take with that document type. As an example, you may have a document type where certain users store documents and set the status on the document information record to "Released" which makes them official documents in your environment. Once released, they are made available for display by all. Therefore, users that create and release these documents need to have a role that allows the activity of "create" for the specific document type. Users that display the documents need a role that allows the activity of "display."

> **Example**
>
> **Desired Security:** A user should have only display access to the document type DRW.
>
> **Settings:** In the authorization object C_DRAW_TCD, the activity Display (03) and document type DRW are maintained in the person's user role.
>
> This will give the user display access to document information records of document type DRW. No other rights will be available.

Fields, values, and descriptions for authorization object C_DRAW_TCD are shown in Table 6.1. When reviewing the table, take note of what activities are available. This will give you an idea of how you can restrict or provide access. Think about how these activities should be combined with the document types you are using.

Fields	Values	Description
ACTVT (Activity)	01	Create
	02	Change
	03	Display
	06	Delete
	19	Maintain number range object
DOKAR (Document Type)	-	The selected activities can be executed for the maintained document types

Table 6.1 Fields, Values, and Descriptions for the Authorization Object C_DRAW_TCD

6.2.2 Authorization Object C_DRAW_TCS — Status Dependent Authorization

Using authorization object C_DRAW_TCS, you can control whether a user can process a document information record based on a combination of activity, document type, and status. This authorization object takes the authorization object C_DRAW_TCD and adds the element of status. You will use this authorization object when you need to use status to restrict access or activities that can be executed.

Example

Desired Security: A user should be able to access only document information records of document type DRW after they have reached a status of "Released" (FR).

Settings: In the authorization object C_DRAW_TCS, the following settings are maintained in the person's user role:

▶ Activity = 03
▶ Document type = DRW
▶ Status = FR (Released)

This gives the user display access to document information records of document type DRW with a status of "Released" (FR). No other rights will be available.

Fields, values, and descriptions for authorization object C_DRAW_TCS are shown in Table 6.2. As with authorization object C_DRAW_TCD, you will want to note the possible combinations of activity, document type, and status.

Fields	Values	Description
ACTVT (Activity)	01	Create
	02	Change
	03	Display
	06	Delete
DOKAR (Document Type)	-	The selected activities can be executed for the maintained document types
STATUS (Document Status)	-	List of statuses during/at which the user has access to perform activities against the associated document types

Table 6.2 Fields, Values, and Descriptions for the Authorization Object C_DRAW_TCS

6.2.3   Authorization Object C_DRAW_STA — Document Status

Using authorization object C_DRAW_STA, you can define which statuses a user may set for a given document type. This authorization object is useful when you want to restrict which statuses a user can set on a document information record. As explained in the example that follows, you may for example want to restrict the releasing of a document information record to a specific group of individuals. This authorization object will allow you to do this.

Example

Desired Security: Document type DRW has a simple status network that progresses in the following manner:

In-Work (IW) -> Pending Approval (PA) -> Approved (AP)

Any user may move the status from In-Work to Pending Approval. However, only a specific group of key users may set the status of Approved. Security should restrict access accordingly.

Settings: In the authorization object C_DRAW_STA, the document type should be DRW and the document status should include IW and PA. These settings are maintained in a person's user role.

This will allow the affected users to move the status from In-Work to Pending Approval, but they will not have access to set the status of the document information record to Approved.

Fields, values, and descriptions for authorization object C_DRAW_STA are shown in Table 6.3. When reviewing the table, think about how you will combine document type and document status to create the security you require.

Fields	Values	Description
DOKAR (Document Type)	-	Document type to control which statuses can be set
DOKST (Document Status)	-	List of statues to be allowed for the document type

Table 6.3   Fields, Values, and Descriptions for the Authorization Object C_DRAW_STA

6.2.4   Authorization Object C_DRAW_BGR — Authorization Group

Using authorization object C_DRAW_BGR, you can restrict access to document information records based on authorization group. This is often used when you want to set up project-type authorizations. As the example that follows explains, when you have groups of individuals working on projects throughout a company, you can restrict access to the documents the project groups are generating by using the authorization group.

Desired Security: A company has a special development project called "Project 150." Only certain users should have access to the documents associated with this project. Therefore, for document information records associated with this project, the authorization group should always be set to P150.

Settings: In the authorization object C_DRAW_BGR, the field BEGRU has the value P150 in the person's user role.

This will limit access to the document information records to those persons who have the correct authorization group maintained in their role.

Fields, values, and descriptions for authorization object C_DRAW_BGR are shown in Table 6.4. If a user should have access to an authorization group, a role for that authorization group must be created and added to the user's profile.

Fields	Values	Description
BEGRU (Authorization Group)	0000 – ZZZZ	Used to further restrict authorizations for document maintenance

Table 6.4 Fields, Values, and Descriptions for the Authorization Object C_DRAW_BGR

6.2.5 Authorization Object C_DRAD_OBJ — Object Link

Using authorization object C_DRAD_OBJ, you can control the ability to add, change, display, or delete object links on a document information record for a document type at a specific status. You can use this when you want to restrict the maintenance of object links on a document information record to a certain group of individuals. This is often used because of what an object link can signify and communicate to others. Object links are visible in other transactions in the SAP system, and someone may be looking for document links to identify documents that can be used for a certain purpose.

> **Example**
>
> **Desired Security:** During the lifecycle of a document information record, material masters are associated through the Object link tab. When the document information record reaches a status of "Released" (FR), no user should be able to create, change, or delete the link.
>
> **Settings:** In the authorization object C_DRAD_OBJ, the following settings are maintained in the person's user role:
>
> ▶ Activity = 03
>
> ▶ Document type = DRW
>
> ▶ Status = FR (Released)
>
> This will allow the user to display object links on the document information record. No other activities will be possible.

Fields, values, and descriptions for authorization object C_DRAD_OBJ are shown in Table 6.5. You need to identify the object link type you are working with before working with this authorization object. This is required data in the field DOKOB.

Fields	Values	Description
ACTVT (Activity)	01	Create
	02	Change
	03	Display
	06	Delete
DOKOB (Object)	-	You must enter the database table for the objects here (for example MARA, for material record)
STATUS (Document Status)	-	Enter the status of the document information record when object links should be controlled

Table 6.5 Fields, Values, and Descriptions for the Authorization Object C_DRAD_OBJ

6.2.6   Authorization Object C_DRAW_DOK — Document Access

Using authorization object C_DRAW_DOK, you can grant access to display, but restrict the ability to change an original file associated with a document information record. This can be used in situations where you want to grant access to change document information record data, but not the associated original files.

> **Example**
>
> **Desired Security:** For document type DRW, a user should have access only to display (but not change) an original file associated with the document information record.
>
> **Settings:** In the authorization object C_DRAW_DOK, the following settings are maintained in the person's user role:
>
> ▶ Activity = 53
>
> ▶ Document type = DRW
>
> This will allow the user to display any original files associated with the document information record. No other activities will be allowed.

Fields, values, and description for authorization object C_DRAW_DOK is shown in Table 6.6. When reviewing the table, pay close attention to the activities that can be restricted.

Fields	Values	Description
ACTVT (Activity)	52	Change application start
	53	Display application start
	54	Display archive application
	55	Change archive application
	56	Display archive
	57	Store archive
DOKAR (Document Type)	-	Document type to allow access to original files

Table 6.6 Fields, Values, Description for the Authorization Object C_DRAW_DOK

6.2.7 Authorization Object C_DRZA_TCD — Activities for Recipient Lists

Using authorization object C_DRZA_TCD, you can set which activities a user is allowed to perform for recipient lists. This is used when working with distribution orders.

Example

Desired Security: A user requires full access when working with distribution orders.

Settings: In the authorization object C_DRZA_TCD, the activity "*" is maintained.

All activities will then be available to the user when working with distribution orders and recipient lists.

Fields, values, and descriptions for authorization object C_DRZA_TCD are shown in Table 6.7. Activities that can be used for restricting or granting access to distribution orders and recipient lists are identified.

Fields	Values	Description
ACTVT (Activity)	01	Create
	02	Change
	03	Display
	06	Delete (only own recipient lists)
	41	Delete (administrator)
	A9	Send (start distribution with recipient list)

Table 6.7 Fields, Values, and Descriptions for the Authorization Object C_DRAW_DOK

6.2.8   Authorization Object C_DRZI_TCD — Distribution Order

Using authorization object C_DRZI_TCD, you can limit parts order processing when working with distribution orders, by only allowing display of the distribution log, but granting no other access.

Example

Desired Security: A user should only be able to display the distribution log, and have no other access.

Settings: In the authorization object C_DRZI_TCD, activity "03" is maintained.

The user will only have access to display the distribution log.

Fields, values, and descriptions for authorization object C_DRZI_TCD are shown in Table 6.8. Activities that can be used for restricting or granting access to the distribution log are identified.

Fields	Values	Description
ACTVT (Activity)	01	Start the distribution manually from the distribution log
	02	Start the distribution again from the distribution log
	03	Display the distribution log
	04	Confirm receipt
	05	Confirm output
	06	Ignore distribution order
	07	Display mail from the distribution log
	08	Delete temporary files from the application server

Table 6.8 Fields, Values, and Descriptions for the Authorization Object C_DRAW_DOK

6.3   Use of Access Control Lists

As of SAP ERP 2005, the use of ACLs is standard in SAP DMS. Previously, this functionality was available through the use of SAP Easy Document Management. To implement ACL capabilities in earlier releases, you must follow the instructions outlined in SAP OSS Note 798504.

Using ACLs, you can control which users, groups of users, roles, or HR objects have access to a document information record. This is an additional check on top of the checks performed through standard authorization objects.

With ACLs, you can give control to a user to decide who should have access to a document information record. This is an important concept that was not available in earlier releases of SAP software. It is often used when working with project groups where you give a project group the ability to restrict access to the document information records they are creating without generating additional roles and going through the process of adding these roles to a user's profile. Earlier in the chapter, we discussed the use of authorization groups. This is the classic method used to fulfill this requirement. However, it has the downside that a lot of roles and user profiles must be updated. Using ACLs involves much less maintenance effort.

To further explain the use of ACLs, let's look at an example scenario.

Example

Joe S. is the owner of document information record 10000000315/ZCH/000/00. At this point in time, many individuals have access to this record because of the authorizations assigned in their user roles.

However, access to this document information record needs to be restricted due to the nature of its content. Joe S. could create a new authorization group and request a new user role to accomplish this, but it would be much easier to add an ACL to the document information record. This way, he can specifically select which users he wants to add and what privileges they will have.

To create an ACL, he will select the tab AUTHORIZATIONS in the document information record. He will then be asked if he wants to create document-specific authorizations. He answers yes, and as shown in Figure 6.1, he will be brought to the tab where he can start adding users, user groups, roles, and HR objects that should have access to the document information record.

To add a user, he will click on the plus icon in the toolbar. This will insert a new row.

For this document information record, he wants Christian H. to have Read access to the document information record. As shown in Figure 6.2, he will configure the following settings to achieve the desired security:

▶ Type of Auth. Obj. = User

▶ ID = CUS00007T (his user ID)

▶ Activity = Read

When the configuration is saved, Christian H. will have only read or display access to the document information record. If he attempts to enter into change mode, he will receive a message that he does not have the correct authorizations.

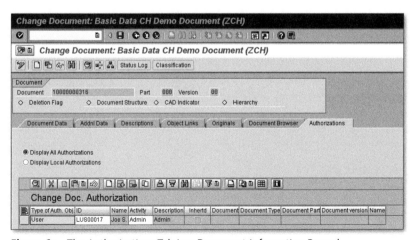

Figure 6.1 The Authorizations Tab in a Document Information Record

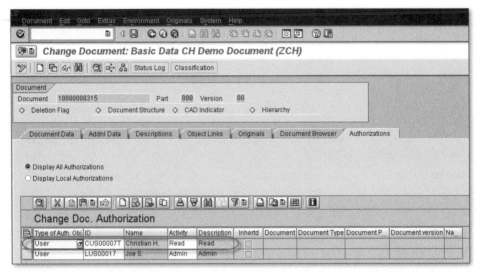

Figure 6.2 Addition of Christian H. to Document Information as Someone Who Has Read Access

Beyond assigning a single user to a document information record, you can also assign a user group, role, or HR object.

A number of activities exist that define the level of security a user can be assigned using an ACL. These are described in Table 6.9.

Activity	Description
Admin	Gives users full access to display, change, rename, copy, and delete documents and linked files.
Delete	Allows users to delete a document.
WriteFile	Allows users to create, delete, and change originals, and to change metadata. The document cannot be deleted.
Write	Allows users to change documents. Deletion is not allowed. Changing a document includes editing and saving an original as well as changing the metadata.
ReadFile	Allows users to display metadata and originals. The original can be exported but can't be changed or deleted.
Read	Allows users to display metadata. Changes are not possible.
NoAuth	No authorizations are assigned.

Table 6.9 Activities that Can Be Assigned through an ACL

Using ACLs is very helpful when you want to manage document information records at a very granular level, but do not want the overhead and additional time required to generate new roles.

6.4 Customer-Specific Authorization Checks

If the standard SAP authorization objects do not address all of your security requirements, you can use also use BAdI DOCUMENT_AUTH01 to add customer-specific authorization checks. For example, you may have a business requirement that is so specific that it can only be addressed through a custom authorization check. For example, you might want to check an attribute on a material master to which the document information record is linked. If the attribute has a certain value, only certain users are allowed to view the document information record. There might be a customer table that defines the attributes and the users that are allowed to view the document information record.

You will find further information about this topic in the chapter on BAdIs and user exits, Chapter 10.

6.5 Summary

In this chapter, we covered the topic of SAP DMS security. Specifically, you were asked to define your security requirements, including when and whether to allow users access to sensitive document records. You then learned about the standard SAP authorization objects and other methods used to control access. Each was covered with a description and example of use. With this information, you can now develop a number of strategies to control access to documents.

In the next chapter, Chapter 7, we will cover the different frontends that are available for SAP DMS.

This chapter reviews the different frontends that are available for SAP DMS.

7 Frontends to SAP DMS

Several different frontends are available for SAP DMS, including Web Documents, SAP Easy DMS, and portal iViews. A *frontend* simply provides a different view for the user to perform the same activities that they would in the SAP GUI. Each frontend offers a different set of benefits and capabilities. As an example, Web Documents offers simplified access to SAP DMS through a web browser. Many users enjoy working through a web browser instead of using the SAP GUI because of the simplicity and familiarity of the browser.

All of the frontends use the same SAP DMS configuration, which is minimal. When your SAP DMS configuration is complete, you can start working with the different frontends. Let's now look at each frontend in detail.

7.1 Web Documents

SAP provides a tool for managing document information records via a web browser, known as Web Documents. This tool is often used when a business is looking for a user interface that is simpler than the SAP GUI. For example, your business may have a set of users who do not execute any activities in the SAP GUI beyond SAP DMS functions. Therefore, they will not need to be trained on how to use the SAP GUI and can instead get to all of the functionality they require through a web browser.

Some of the actions you can complete via a web browser using Web Documents include the following:

▶ Find document information records
▶ Display and edit document information records
▶ Create new document information records

- ▶ Update additional attributes, object links, and language-dependent descriptions on document information records
- ▶ Change original files
- ▶ Execute searches by basic document attributes, classification, full text, and linked objects

As you can see, working in the web browser, it is possible to perform almost all of the actions you can perform working in the SAP GUI. Actions you can't perform via web browser include displaying the status network, opening the product structure browser, or displaying the change history. Even though these functions are not available, the Web Documents application remains a very attractive tool for a certain set of users.

7.1.1 The Technology Behind Web Documents

Web Documents is developed using Business Server Page (BSP) technology. You can review the underlying programming of the Web Documents tool through Transaction SE80 (Object Navigator). As shown in Figure 7.1, in the navigator select object type BSP APPLICATION and application CVAW_ENTIRE.

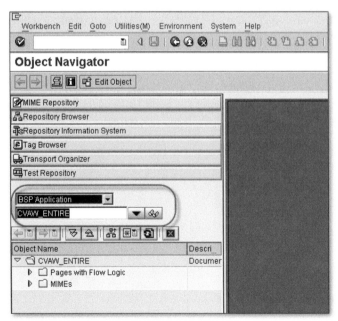

Figure 7.1 The Object Navigator

The key activity you can perform from here is launching the application. Right-click on the folder labeled CVAW_ENTIRE and select the option TEST. This will launch your browser and you will be asked to log in. Enter your username and password. Launching Web Documents via the Object Navigator will cut down on the time spent looking for the correct URL to the application.

7.1.2 Configuration of Web Documents

The Web Documents tool is configured via the SAP IMG. It is located in the same area where all other document management configuration is completed. Specifically, the configuration is completed by executing actions under SET UP WEB DOCUMENTS (BSP).

Configuration consists of two steps. First, you must define which document types you want to make available in Web Documents. Then for each document type you define the following:

1. Which field groups, or sections, of the document of the information record should be available.
   - Possible field groups include:
     - Document Key
     - Document Data
     - Additional Data
     - Object Links
     - Originals
     - Description
2. Define which functions will be available to the user.
   - Possible functions include:
     - Display Status Log
     - Display Versions
     - Display Hierarchy
     - Send

     – Delete

     – Create New Version

3. Define the thumbnail image application.

Now that you are familiar with the configuration required for Web Documents, we can take a look at an example configuration.

Example Configuration

The first item to complete is defining which document types will be available for use with Web Documents, as shown in Figure 7.2. In the example, the document types for engineering design drawings, archive footage, specifications, and others will be available via Web Documents.

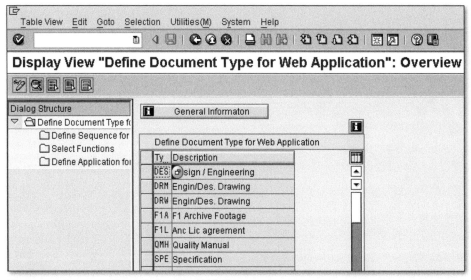

Figure 7.2 Document Types Defined for Web Documents

Selecting the document type DES, you can drill down to review and change the sequence for fields groups, as shown in Figure 7.3. For a specific document type, you can view or specify the order for the field groups DOCUMENT KEY, DOCUMENT DATA, ADDITIONAL DATA, OBJECT LINKS, ORIGINALS, and DESCRIPTION. These relate to sections or tabs on the document information record.

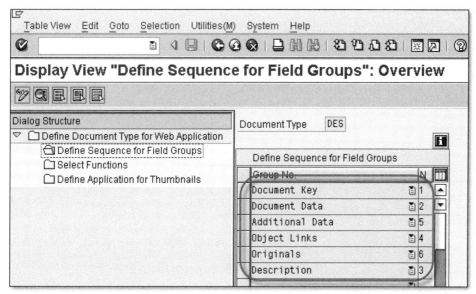

Figure 7.3 Defining the Sequence for Field Groups

You can also take a look at what functions will be available for the document type you selected, as shown in Figure 7.4. For the document type DES, the functions DISPLAY STATUS LOG, DISPLAY VERSIONS, and CREATE NEW VERSION will be available.

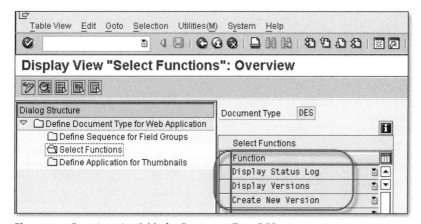

Figure 7.4 Functions Available for Document Type DES

The last item you need to configure is whether you want to define an application for thumbnails. Doing so will make Web Documents display a small thumbnail image when one is available as an original file associated to the document information record. An example is shown in Figure 7.5.

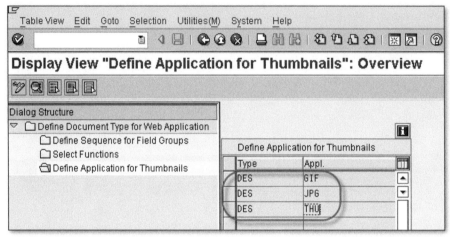

Figure 7.5 Defining an Application for Thumbnails

This completes the required configuration. You can now begin using the Web Documents.

7.1.3 An Example of Working in Web Documents

We'll now go through a simple example of working in Web Documents by reviewing how to execute a search. After the search is complete, you will update the document information record description and display the original files that are attached to it. Remember that this is meant to be a simple example for you to learn basic navigation and actions. When you have completed this exercise, it will be intuitive how to execute additional functions.

Open Web Documents and Log in

Open Web Documents in your web browser and log in. The initial page of Web Documents is shown in Figure 7.6. From this page, you can do the following:

- ▶ Open the stack (recent documents information records processed)
- ▶ Find document information records
- ▶ Open past search results
- ▶ Display or change a specific document information record
- ▶ Create a new document information record

For our example, click on the FIND link.

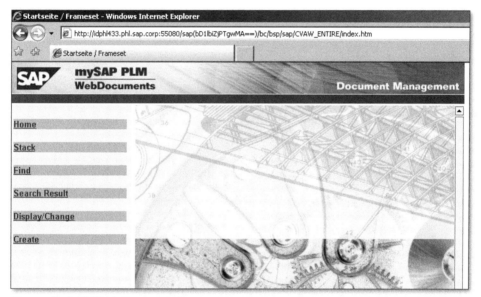

Figure 7.6 Initial Web Documents Page

On the Find page, as shown in Figure 7.7, you can execute a variety of searches. This includes searching by basic document attributes, classification, object links, and full text.

For this example, we'll execute a search for document information records linked to a certain material master. For search criteria, you would enter the document type you want search on in the document type field. When the search criterion has been entered, click on the START SEARCH button.

Figure 7.7   The Search Screen in Web Documents

Next, the search results are returned, as shown in Figure 7.8. Click on the pencil
icon next to the document information record you are planning to change.

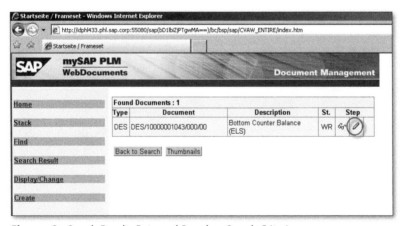

Figure 7.8   Search Results Returned Based on Search Criteria

As shown in Figure 7.9, the screen for changing the document information record displays. From here, you can change a variety of elements on the document information record. Based on the configuration you have set up, this can include:

▶ Basic data attributes

▶ Language-dependent descriptions

▶ Additional attributes

▶ Original files

On the document information record you opened, update one of the attributes. This can be something simple, such as updating the description. When complete, click on the Save button to save your changes.

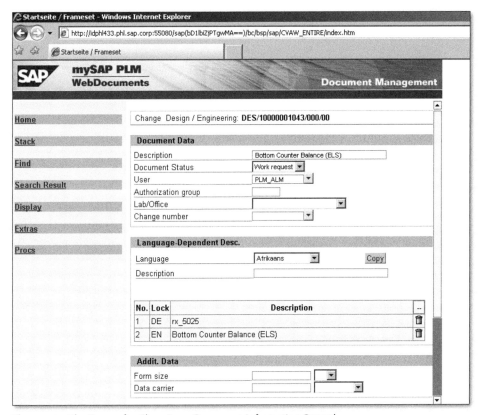

Figure 7.9 The Screen for Changing a Document Information Record

This concludes the example, and the section on Web Documents. As mentioned earlier, Web Documents is an excellent tool for users you may not want to train to use the SAP GUI. It is also a good tool to have in your arsenal of items to deploy to meet business requirements. From the standpoint of configuration and rollout, it is easy to use and has low impact.

7.2   SAP Easy DMS

SAP Easy DMS is another frontend to SAP DMS you can use. It is actually a Microsoft Windows application that is installed on a local machine. As the name states, it offers functionality that makes the task of managing documents easier for users. Its functionality includes:

▶ Check in, check out, and save documents directly in Microsoft Office applications (Word, Excel, etc.)

▶ Use private and public folders for document management

▶ Drag and drop documents to initiate document storage

▶ Search for documents outside of the SAP GUI

▶ Edit classification data

▶ Create and edit objects links

Users like SAP Easy DMS because they do not need to initiate an SAP GUI session to store a document. Instead, they can store documents directly from an application, such as Microsoft Word, or by using the drag and drop functionality.

As an example of the SAP Easy DMS interface, Figure 7.10 shows the dialog box used to store a document. You can see that based on DOCUMENT TYPE, you have to fill a certain set of fields, including the fields in the ADDITIONAL DATA area. When completed, a document information record will be created in the SAP system. The file will also be stored in the selected content server.

Figure 7.11 shows a folder structure created in SAP Easy DMS. The use of folders in SAP Easy DMS is one its main selling points and benefits. It allows users to work with the familiar concept of folders for organizing documents. The folder structures are actually maintained in the backend SAP system as document structures.

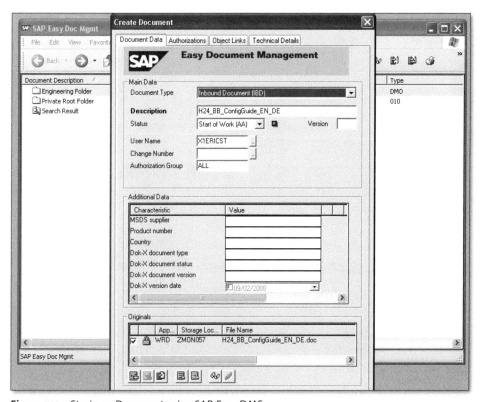

Figure 7.10 Storing a Document using SAP Easy DMS

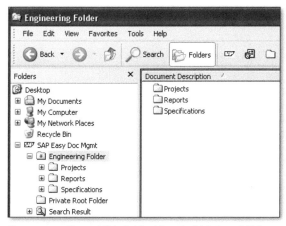

Figure 7.11 Figure 7.11 Folder View in SAP Easy DMS

7.2.1   SAP Easy DMS Installation

You can download SAP Easy DMS from the SAP Service Marketplace. After the download has completed, installing SAP Easy DMS is as simple as extracting the files contained in the ZIP archive and executing the setup program. After installation, you should reboot the computer.

7.2.2   SAP Easy DMS Configuration

SAP Easy DMS works with the existing SAP DMS configuration, so no additional configuration required. When you store a document using SAP Easy DMS, you are presented with the same document types, additional attributes, and object link possibilities as if you were working in the SAP GUI.

7.2.3   Effort for Implementing SAP DMS

Because SAP Easy DMS uses the backend SAP DMS configuration, the actual effort for rolling out SAP Easy DMS as an application is relatively straight forward. As long as SAP DMS is configured as you want it, you can immediately begin using SAP Easy DMS. Most of the effort is then spent on the business rules of how the tool should be used and how folders should be structured.

7.3   SAP DMS Portal iView

You can use the SAP portal to access documents that are managed by the SAP system. Specific iViews are provided with the business package DMS Connector for Knowledge Management (KM). The benefit is that you can add this functionality as additional information you are able to access via your portal. The portal is meant to be the one place users can go to for information, instead of having a wide variety of websites and applications to navigate.

The system requirements for using the business package for DMS are as follows:

▸ **Portal**: SAP NetWeaver 2004 (stack 10) or SAP NetWeaver® 7.0 (or later)

▸ **Backend system**: SAP R/3 (release 4.6C and later) or SAP ERP ECC 6.0

▸ **Other**: Plug-In 2003.1 (or later)

7.4   Summary

In this chapter we covered three different frontends to SAP DMS:

▶ Web Documents: A web-based user interface

▶ SAP Easy DMS: A Microsoft Windows application

▶ SAP DMS Portal: iViews available to make SAP DMS visible in your portal

These frontends are often helpful when you need to provide users with a different entry point into SAP DMS other than through the standard SAP GUI.

Each frontend has its own benefits and capabilities, and is relatively simple to get up and running.

It's important to remember that the frontends use the existing SAP DMS configuration. Therefore, when you have completed your SAP DMS configuration, it is possible to immediately begin working with the different frontends.

In the next chapter, Chapter 8, you will learn about integrating your CAD system to SAP.

Using SAP-provided integration interfaces, you can store and manage CAD data in SAP DMS. This chapter takes a closer look at how to accomplish this.

8 Integrating a CAD System to SAP DMS

In this chapter you will learn about integrating CAD systems into SAP DMS. First, you will learn which interfaces are available. This will give you an idea if it is possible to integrate a specific CAD system into SAP DMS. You will then learn about the capabilities and benefits of integrating a CAD system to SAP DMS. Next, we will introduce you to the SAP CAD Desktop and a walk you through a simple sample CAD integration scenario.

Note that this chapter is meant to be an introduction to a broad topic; in fact, there could easily be a separate chapter for explaining how to work with each CAD interface. This is because each CAD package is unique and has its own set of rules on how it functions. Providing this detailed information is, however, beyond the scope of this book. Therefore, you should select the CAD interface you intend to use and simply start working with it. You can also gather good information from the partners who work directly with SAP to develop the interfaces. They have a wealth of knowledge and provide excellent support during implementation.

8.1 Available SAP CAD Integration Interfaces

Listed in Table 8.1 are CAD systems that have a direct integration interface to SAP DMS. You can purchase interfaces directly from SAP, or from the respective SAP development partner.

CAD Interface	Development Partners
AutoCAD	Cideon
AutoDesk Inventor	Cideon
CATIA V4	Cenit
CATIA V5	Cenit
I-deas	Tesis
ME10	DSC
Medusa	DSC
Microstation	Cideon
Pro/Engineer	.riess
Solid Edge	Cideon
SolidWorks	Cideon
Unigraphics	DSC

Table 8.1 CAD Interfaces Available with Development Partners

8.2 Capabilities and Benefits of CAD Interfaces

Because each CAD tool is unique, there will be different benefits and capabilities to each interface. However, certain standard capabilities and benefits exist because the CAD integration interfaces have been designed to provide a similar set of capabilities.

8.2.1 Capabilities

Typically, each CAD integration interface will provide the following capabilities:

▶ Secure storage of CAD data.

▶ Execution of relevant SAP DMS transactions that support the management of CAD data, directly from the CAD tool.

▶ Maintenance of the structure and relationships when storing or changing the CAD data, if you are using a CAD tool (e.g., CATIA V5) that maintains a structure and relationship between models.

▶ Use of SAP engineering change management tools on stored CAD data.

- Creation, changing, and display of supporting master data objects such as material masters and BOMs.

- Generation of a neutral file of the stored CAD data to allow viewing of data by users who do not have a CAD application.

8.2.2 Benefits

There are a number of benefits you can expect to obtain when using one of the CAD integration interfaces. They are as follows:

- CAD data is secure and updates are controlled.

- You can use SAP engineering change management tools to control data creation and updates. You can also create a more formal process that involves workflow and approvals for managing the lifecycle of the data.

- Data is visible to others who may need access for decision making.

- Storage of CAD data can be the initiation point for the creation of material masters and BOMs.

- Once CAD data is stored, additional processes can be triggered, such as an approval or review workflow.

- Neutral files can be generated for viewing by users who do not have access to the CAD application.

- You move away from managing files to actually managing the process for creation and change of CAD data.

8.3 SAP CAD Desktop

As shown in Figure 8.1, the CAD Desktop (Transaction: CDESK) is the tool provided by SAP for managing CAD data in SAP DMS after it is transferred from the CAD application. It lets you manage single documents and document structures for CAD applications that use an assembly type structure. Some of its basic functions include:

- Creating a document information record for a model or drawing being stored.

- Changing the status of a document information record.

- Checking in and checking out original files.

▶ Creating a material master for a given document information record.

▶ Creating a BOM based on document structure and related materials.

▶ Changing data with relation to an engineering change master.

As mentioned, these are the basic functions of the CAD Desktop. It has many other capabilities that are best understood and demonstrated by using one of the CAD integration interfaces.

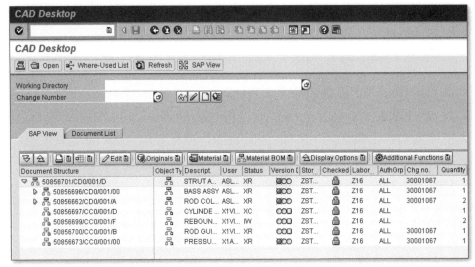

Figure 8.1 View of the CAD Desktop

From a technical standpoint, communication between the CAD application and the CAD Desktop is accomplished through remote function calls (RFCs). This allows transfer or creation of data in the SAP DMS system directly from the CAD application. You do not necessarily need to open the SAP GUI to execute functions. You can work comfortably in your CAD application.

8.4 Example CAD Integration Scenario

To give you an idea of the steps a user would need to take when working with one of the SAP CAD integration interfaces, we will provide you with an example.

You own a company that designs bicycles. All new bicycles start with an initial design in your CAD application. Data that is generated in your CAD application needs to be stored in SAP DMS for a variety of reasons, including secure storage and the ability to share the data with others in remote offices.

You would take the following steps to create and store the CAD data into SAP DMS.

1. **Create the CAD data representing the new bicycle design.** In your CAD application, create the CAD data. This could include models and drawings.

2. **From the CAD application, execute the menu item to store CAD data in SAP DMS.** At a certain maturity level, you will store the generated CAD data back into SAP DMS. Through a menu item in the CAD application, transfer the CAD data from the CAD application to the SAP CAD Desktop.

3. **Create document information records.** For each CAD model or drawing, create a corresponding document information record. From the CAD Desktop, you can select the newly transferred CAD data and create the document information records in bulk. Fill in all required attributes.

4. **Create material masters.** For each part of the bicycle assembly, create a material master. The material master created here will be the starting definition for each part. This will be extended at a later point to include information such as how to manufacture, procure, or sell the part.

5. **Create a BOM.** For the assembly, create a bill of material. This is the parts list or structure of what parts go into building the bicycle. It is made from the material masters that were created in the above step.

6. **Check in CAD data.** Check in the CAD data to move it from your local storage to the SAP DMS content server. This will make it possible for you to share the data with others.

7. **Exit the SAP CAD Desktop.** Exit the SAP CAD Desktop to return to your CAD application.

8. **Process complete, close CAD application.** You can now close your CAD application; the process is complete. You can later retrieve the CAD data that was stored into SAP DMS and continue making modifications.

8.5   CAD Data Migration

When implementing one of the CAD interfaces, you will want to consider how you will handle data migration of existing CAD data into SAP DMS. This can be a simple process or a very complex one. As an example of a simple data migration, let's say that you are interfacing Autocad to SAP DMS and you want to migrate all of your legacy Autocad files into SAP DMS. For Autocad, there are no relationships between each file. Therefore, it is a fairly simple process to create a new document information record for each file and add the Autocad file as an original file. As an example of a complex data migration process, let's say that you are working with a CAD tool such as CATIA V5 or UG NX and using assembly structures. This means that you will have to carefully load the CAD data into SAP DMS so that relationships between files are maintained and the assembly structure remains intact. This can be done on a one-by-one basis, or with tools that are developed by some of the CAD partners mentioned previously in Table 8.1.

8.6 Summary

This chapter provided you a brief introduction to the topic of integrating a CAD system into SAP DMS. We covered what SAP CAD integration interfaces are available, and reviewed some of the capabilities and benefits of integrating your CAD system to SAP DMS. We also took a quick look at the SAP CAD Desktop, and at a typical CAD integration scenario.

In the next chapter, Chapter 9, we will cover the creation of a simple document approval process using SAP Workflow.

This chapter provides instructions on how to set up a simple approval process using SAP Workflow based on a document status change.

9 Simple Document Approval Process using SAP Workflow

An approval process for a document information record can be created as simple or complex as needed. In this chapter, we will look at the fundamental steps and tools to create a basic document approval process using SAP Workflow. When you understand these methods, you can expand the process to include more intricate working models.

9.1 The Workflow Scenario

For our scenario, a document information record being set to the status of "Review" initiates a workflow notification that is sent to a reviewer. Within the workflow notification is a link to the document information record, allowing the reviewer instant access to the data. If it is approved, the reviewer sets the status of the document information record to "Released." If it is not approved, the reviewer sets the status back to "In-Work." A workflow notification is sent to the initiator of the workflow with the results of the review.

9.2 Required SAP DMS and Workflow Configuration

Some SAP DMS configuration is required before proceeding with workflow set-up. The requirements are as follows:

▶ Create a new document type SMA (Simple Approval Demo) with a status network of In-Work, Review, and Released.

> **Note**
>
> Instead of creating a new document type from scratch, you can copy one of the standard document types that are delivered with the SAP system, such as DRW. After the copy, you will need to modify the status network.

▶ Allow users to change the status of the document information record from In-Work to Review, Review to In-Work, and Review to Released.

After you have completed the required configuration, you can move on to the SAP Workflow system. The SAP Workflow system must be configured for this example to work. Because this guide does not focus on SAP Workflow, the steps for configuration are not covered here. To check whether basic SAP Workflow settings are complete, execute Transaction SWU3 (Automatic Workflow Customizing). If settings are not complete, refer to SAP Help for the steps to complete them.

9.3 Creating the Workflow Definition

This section covers the steps to create the workflow definition. The workflow definition encompasses how the workflow will be triggered and what steps or tasks will happen during the workflow.

9.3.1 Execute Transaction PFTC (Task: Maintain)

Transaction PFTC is used to define the workflow you are building. Because this will be a multi-step workflow definition, select task type "Workflow template" and click on the CREATE button, as shown in Figure 9.1. This is the first step in creating a workflow definition.

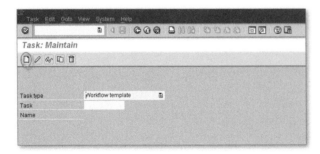

Figure 9.1 Task Maintain Entry Screen

9.3.2 Enter Information on the Basic Data Tab of the Workflow Definition

The next step in creating a workflow definition is to fill in the information on the BASIC DATA tab. This information is important because it specifies how you will search for the workflow definition and identify that it is a release workflow definition. The field values you will enter on the BASIC DATA tab are displayed in Table 9.1. The fields, as illustrated in Figure 9.2, are straightforward. The field ABBR. is a short abbreviation given to the workflow definition. The field NAME provides a short description for the workflow definition. The field RELEASE STATUS identifies what state the workflow definition is in.

Field	Value
Abbr.	ZSIMAPPR
Name	Simple Document Approval Process
Released status	Released

Table 9.1 Basic Data Tab Field Values

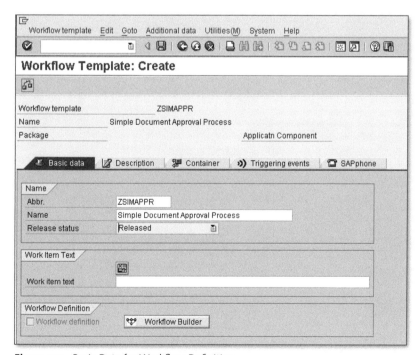

Figure 9.2 Basic Data for Workflow Definition

9.3.3 Create New Container Element

After you've completed the basic data tab, the next step is to create a new container element. The *container element* is like a vessel and specifies how data is passed from the triggering event to the workflow and the task. For our example, we are creating a container element for the document information record. When the workflow is triggered by changing the status of the document information record, all of the information about the document information record (e.g., description, owner, status, etc.) will be passed from the event and put into the container element. Therefore, you can work with this data to make decisions in the workflow, such as whether the workflow should be triggered, or who should review it.

To create a new container element, you must first select the CONTAINER tab. Define a new container element, and call it "Document." To do this, click on the toolbar button on the far left of the tab, called CREATE ELEMENT. Enter data as shown in Figure 9.3 and Figure 9.4. This includes providing a name, short description, and object type, and also setting the properties of import/export for the new container element.

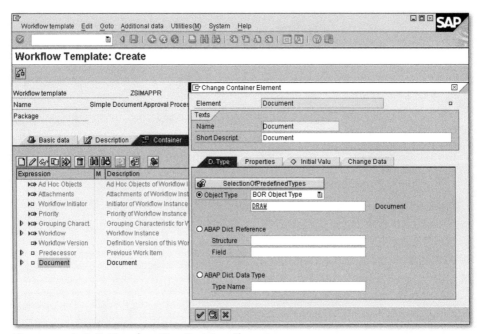

Figure 9.3 Basic Settings for a New Container Element

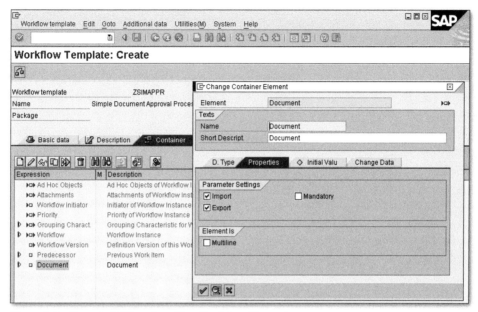

Figure 9.4 Property Settings for a New Container Element

9.3.4 Save the Workflow Definition

After clicking on the SAVE icon, a screen labeled CREATE OBJECT DIRECTORY ENTRY will appear. On this screen, click on the button LOCAL OBJECT. This assigns the new workflow to package $TMP and a new internal number is generated for the workflow definition, as shown in Figure 9.5.

Workflow template	98000501	ZSIMAPPR
Name	Simple Document Approval Process	
Package	$TMP	

Figure 9.5 Workflow Template Number Assigned and Associated to Package $TMP

9.3.5 Add Triggering Event

Select the TRIGGERING EVENTS tab. This is where you will identify how the workflow will start. The workflow you are defining will start when a document information record is changed in some way. We will further refine the starting event at a later point in the process so that the workflow starts for a defined document type and status change.

As shown in Figure 9.6, select an OBJECT CATEGORY of BOR OBJECT TYPE, an OBJECT TYPE DRAW, and EVENT CHANGED. After entering values, click on the far left button in the event creator column to activate the event. This button is currently green, to identify that the triggering event is activated and the workflow will start when this event is raised in the system.

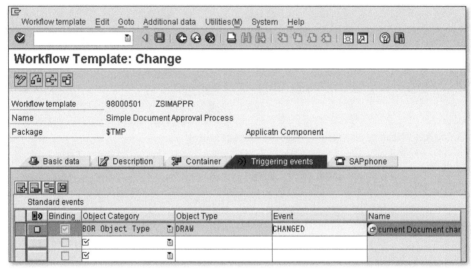

Figure 9.6 Definition of a Workflow Triggering Event

9.3.6 Start the Workflow Builder

The Workflow Builder is where you will define the flow or what tasks will be executed during the workflow. You will also define additional start conditions. This is the first step. To start the Workflow Builder, click on the WORKFLOW BUILDER button.

9.3.7 Set the Additional Start Conditions

Setting additional start conditions will specify that the workflow will only start for a certain document type and status. This is important because a general triggering event was set when the workflow definition was created. This needs to be refined so that it is not triggered every time a document is changed.

To set the additional start conditions, click on the BASIC DATA icon in the Workflow Builder toolbar. Next, select the START EVENTS tab and click on the START CONDITION button, as shown in Figure 9.7.

Figure 9.7 The Start Events Tab

In the condition builder, set the condition DOCUMENT TYPE equal to "SMA" and DOCUMENT STATUS equal to "RV," as shown in Figure 9.8. This workflow will now start only for document type SMA and status RV.

You can use the check function in the condition builder to make sure your condition is set correctly. If it is correct, click on the green check mark button to return to the previous screen. If required, input a transport request. A transport request tracks the changes you are making. Use the back button to return to the main workflow builder screen.

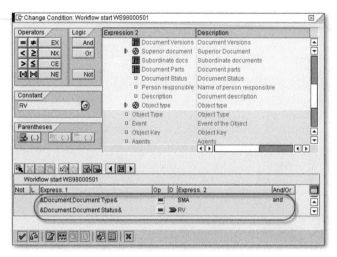

Figure 9.8 The Condition Builder with Conditions Entered

9.3.8 Add Tasks to the Workflow

The next step is adding tasks to the workflow. As shown in Figure 9.9, you can create a new activity by right-clicking on the undefined activity in the main workflow builder screen and selecting CREATE. In the STEP SELECTION screen, select ACTIVITY.

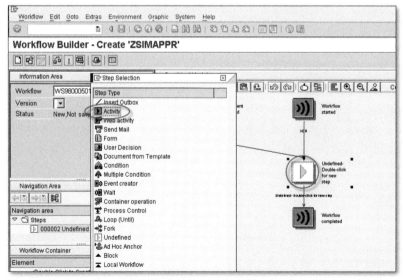

Figure 9.9 Selecting an Undefined Activity and Calling the Step Selection Screen

As shown in Figure 9.10, on the ACTIVITY definition screen, you can select TASK TS7842 and the function COPY AND EDIT TASK.

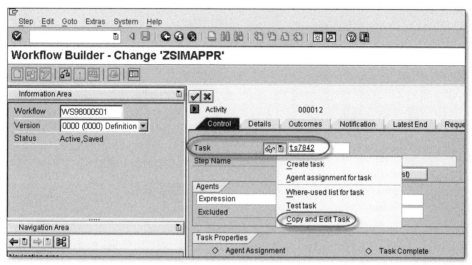

Figure 9.10 The Activity Definition Screen

The next screen that appears is for container elements and binding. Click on the green check mark button to accept the system recommendations.

Another screen will appear with the heading COPY TASK. In the field abbreviation, add a "Z" to the front of DRAW CHANGE. Click on the COPY TASK button.

On the CREATE OBJECT DIRECTORY entry screen, click on the button LOCAL OBJECT. This will place the new task into the development package $TMP and takes you to the main screen for defining the task.

In the work item text, replace the words "was changed" with "Ready for Review." Do not change anything else.

On the TERMINATING EVENTS tab, configure the setting so that the workflow item will terminate or complete when the document is changed. Set element equal to _WI_OBJECT_ID and event equal to CHANGED, as shown in Figure 9.11.

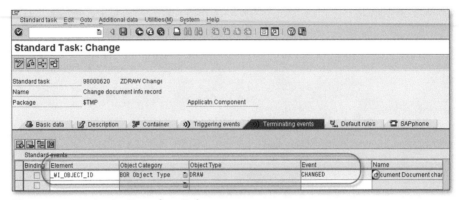

Figure 9.11   Terminating Event for a Task

The new task must be set to be a general task. A *general task* can be executed by anyone in the system. To set the general task, follow the menu path ADDITIONAL DATA • AGENT ASSIGNMENT • MAINTAIN.

As shown in Figure 9.12, select the task and click on the ATTRIBUTES... button. Select GENERAL TASK, and click on the TRANSFER button. Use the BACK button to get back to the main task definition screen. The task can now be executed by every-one in the system. It is also possible to restrict execution of the task to a group of users.

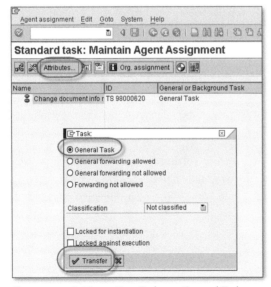

Figure 9.12   Setting a New Task as a General Task

Save the task and use the green arrow button to return to the ACTIVITY definition screen. The new task number will be populated. In this case, the new task number is TS9800620, as shown in Figure 9.13.

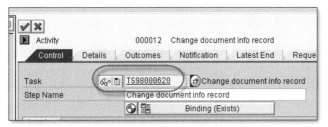

Figure 9.13   The New Task Number Populated

Set the agent to execute the workflow task to the initiator of the workflow. This means that whoever triggers the workflow will receive the notification to review the document. This is a simple scenario and can be configured to be much more complex, such as selecting an agent based on the document type and status.

In the AGENTS area, set the expression to &_WF_INITIATOR&. Click on the green check mark to transfer the task to the workflow definition. Your workflow definition should now look like the one shown in Figure 9.14.

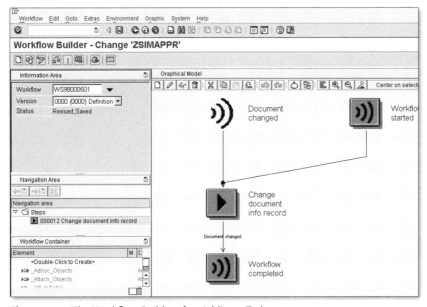

Figure 9.14   The Workflow Builder after Adding a Task

Add another task to the workflow so that the initiator of the workflow is notified when the review process is complete.

Right-click on the element DOCUMENT CHANGED in the workflow builder and select CREATE. From the STEP SELECTION menu, select SEND MAIL. As mentioned previously, an email will be sent after the review is complete.

For the SEND MAIL task definition, on the MAIL tab, enter a RECIPIENT TYPE of "Organizational Object" with an EXPRESSION of "&_WF_INITIATOR&." This way, the workflow initiator will receive notification that the review has been completed. In the SUBJECT field enter "Review Document &DOCUMENT.DOCUMENTNUMBER& Complete." This is the subject line of the notification the reviewer will receive. In the lower text area, enter the message you would like to send. All of this information is shown in Figure 9.15.

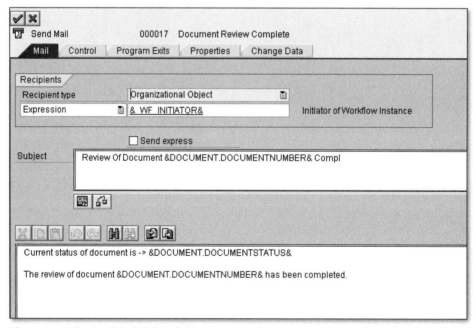

Figure 9.15 The Send Mail Task Definition

To insert dynamic expressions, use the INSERT EXPRESSIONS button in the SUBJECT area.

After entering the information, use the green arrow button to return to the workflow builder. You will be asked to provide a task abbreviation and name. Enter information of your choice. Click on the green checkmark button. On the screen that displays, save the object as a local object. The SEND MAIL task will be transferred to your workflow definition.

9.3.9 Activate the Workflow

You have now completed the workflow definition. The last step is activating the workflow. As shown in Figure 9.16, click on the ACTIVATE button. This will save and activate the workflow in the system.

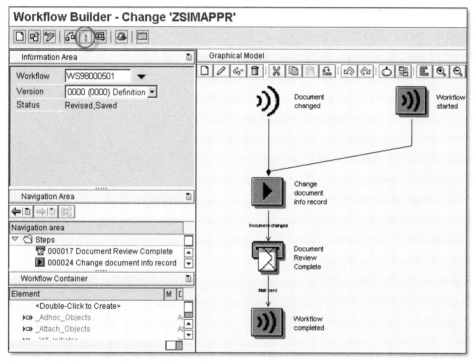

Figure 9.16 Activating the Workflow Definition

9.4 Execute and Test the Workflow

In the system, execute the following steps to test the workflow you built in the previous steps:

1. Execute Transaction CV01N to create a new document information record. On the first screen, enter document type "SMA" and press ⌊Enter⌋.

2. On the next screen, in the DOCUMENT DATA area, enter a short description in the DESCRIPTION field and save the change.

3. Open the new document information record in change mode and set the status to "Review."

4. Open your SAP Business Workplace using Transaction SBWP. In the Inbox, locate the folder WORKFLOW and select it. As shown in Figure 9.17, locate the workflow notification for the document information record that was set to a status of REVIEW. Double-click on the workflow notification to access the document information record.

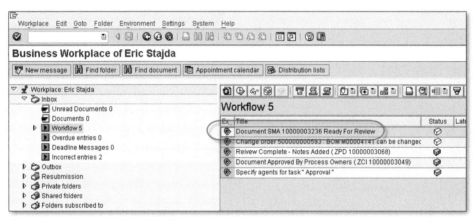

Figure 9.17 Inbox with Workflow Item to Review Document

5. Set the status on the document information record to "Released" and save the change.

6. Select the INBOX folder and update it using the UPDATE icon in the upper left corner of the Inbox toolbar. As shown in Figure 9.18, an email notification appears stating that the document review has been completed. Double-click on the email notification. You will see that the review has been completed, along with the current status of the document.

Figure 9.18 Email Notification that the Review Has Been Completed

9.5   Summary

In this chapter, we provided you with a simple demonstration of the tools and methods for SAP Workflow. You should now understand concepts such as what a triggering event is, and how to build a workflow definition. It is also possible to create much more complex scenarios, such as:

▶ Creating an ad hoc approval process where the approvers are assigned at triggering.

▶ Instead of triggering the workflow by status change, have the workflow manually started through generic object services.

▶ Create a serial approval process, where additional approvers are sent notification after one approved.

▶ Trigger a workflow based on a redline or markup being added.

In the next chapter, Chapter 10, we will take a look at the different BAdIs and user exits available to further customize to SAP DMS.

This chapter reviews SAP DMS BAdIs and users exits, which can be used to expand the standard "out-of-the-box" SAP DMS functionality. Definitions, methods, and example usage are provided.

10   SAP DMS BAdIs and User Exits

SAP has an excellent "out-of-the-box" DMS system that can be configured to meet most business requirements. However, there are cases when additional business rules must be implemented that aren't supported through IMG configuration. In these cases, SAP provides you with a number of BAdIs and user exits that help you to expand the standard functionality of SAP DMS. Throughout this chapter, we'll review the different BAdIs and explain when and why you should use them.

10.1   About SAP BAdIs and User Exits

BAdIs and user exits differ in a number of ways. In terms of age, BAdIs are the newer technology based on ABAP Objects; however, the user exits in the system remain available from earlier releases. One major difference between a BAdI and a user exit is that you can implement a BAdI multiple times. This is not possible with a user exit, because you have only one instance and location to include additional code. SAP also guarantees upward compatibility of BAdI interfaces. This lowers the risk of rework when upgrading to a new release of SAP.

To review a BAdI, use Transaction Business Add-Ins (SE18). Reviewing the available methods, as shown in Figure 10.1, will give you an excellent idea of what is possible.

BAdIs are based on object-oriented programming concepts. It is not necessary to understand object-oriented programming to make use of a BAdI, however. For simplicity, think of a method as a functional module with import and export parameters that is executed at a specific time.

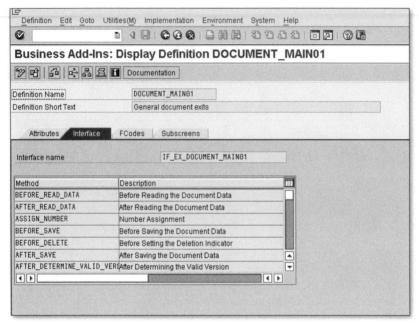

Figure 10.1 Review of Methods for the BAdI DOCUMENT_MAIN01

To review the functionality of a user exit, as shown in Figure 10.2, use Transaction SAP Enhancements (SMOD). You should pay special attention to the available components. They will guide you to the function modules where you can quickly identify where custom code can be placed.

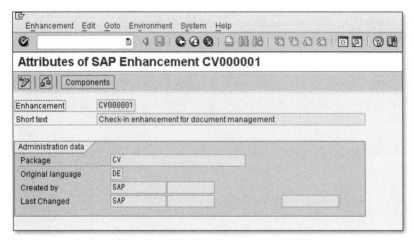

Figure 10.2 Review of User Exit CV000001in Transaction SMOD

We'll review the different BAdIs in detail. For each BAdI, we'll cover available methods, time of execution, and example usage.

10.1.1 BAdI DOCUMENT_MAIN01 - General Document Processing

Using BAdI DOCUMENT_MAIN01, you can carry out customer-specific checks or actions during the process of reading or saving a document information record. This is a key BAdI, and it is used often because it allows you to check or manipulate document information data during these processes.

In Table 10.1, you'll find the available methods, time of execution, and example usages for BAdI DOCUEMTN_MAIN01.

Method	Time Of Execution	Example Usage
Before_Read_Data	Before reading a document information record.	Complete an additional authorization check to make sure that the user has access to display, change, or create.
After_Read_Data	After reading a document information record.	Set lab/office or other default values in the document information record based on the location stored in the user's master record.
Assign_Number	When saving a document information record.	Determine the number to be assigned to the document information record. This replaces GET_NUMBER in program MCDOKZNR.
Before_Save	Before saving a document information record.	Perform a custom check to ensure that the document information record is linked to a material master before allowing the status to move to "Released."
Before_Delete	Before deletion of a document information record.	Check additional rules contained in a Z-table before allowing the document to be deleted.

Table 10.1 Available Methods, Time of Execution, and Example Usage for BAdI DOCUMENT_ MAIN01

Method	Time Of Execution	Example Usage
After_Save	After saving a document information record.	Create a companion material master with the document number as the material number, and link it to the document information record.
After_Determine_Valid_ Version	After a valid version has been determined	Customer-specific check to determine the valid version of the document information record.

Table 10.1 Available Methods, Time of Execution, and Example Usage for BAdI DOCUMENT_ MAIN01 (Cont.)

10.1.2 BAdI DOCUMENT_AUTH01 - Checking Authorization from the DMS

Using BAdI DOCUMENT_AUTH01, you can add customer authorization checks beyond the standard SAP authorization objects. This BAdI allows you to perform multiple additional custom checks to ensure that only an authorized individual gains access to documents. Going beyond standard authorization checks is often required due to business requirements. For an example, you may not want to use authorization groups because of the requirements associated with maintaining roles and assigning these roles to users. Instead, you can develop a custom authorization check that will check a customer table for certain values to confirm that a user can open a document information record.

Available methods, time of execution, and example usage for BAdI DOCUMENT_ AUTH01 are outlined in Table 10.2.

Method	Time Of Execution	Example Usage
Check_Authority	After the following authorization have been checked: C_DRAW_TCD C_DRAW_TCS C_DRAW_DOK	Customer-specific authorization check that goes beyond the checks performed by the standard authorization objects provide by SAP.

Table 10.2 Available Methods, Time of Execution, and Example Usage for BAdI DOCUMENT_ AUTH01

10.1.3 BAdI DOCUMENT_FILES01 - Processing Of Original Application Files

BAdI DOCUMENT_FILES01 allows you to carry out additional customer checks so you can process original files associated to the document information record. This is useful if you require special handling of original files during processing of a document information record. Additional checks can be made during or after assignment, before or after start of the application, and when creating a new version. This gives you an idea of when you can institute special processing instructions.

Available methods, time of execution, and example usage for BAdI DOCUMENT_FILES01 are outlined in Table 10.3.

Method	Time Of Execution	Example Usage
Before_Assign_File	Before assignment of an original application file.	Restrict the type of application file that can be associated to a document information record.
After_Assign_File	After assignment of an original application file.	Configure additional settings in the document information record after successful assignment of an original file.
Before_Start_Appl	Before starting the application that presents the original file.	Uncompress a compressed file before starting the application.
After_Start_Appl	After the presenting application has started.	Delete any temporary files stored on the frontend computer.
Before_Copy_File_Dialog	When you create a new version and the original application files are not checked in before the dialog box for entering a copy path is displayed.	Determine the file name for the new version.

Table 10.3 Available Methods, Time of Execution, and Example Usage for BAdI DOCUMENT_FILES01

Method	Time Of Execution	Example Usage
After_Copy_File_Dialog	When you create a new version, and the original application files are not checked in after the original application files were copied.	Confirm that an original application file exists.
Generate_Copy_File_Name	When you create a new version, and the original application files are not checked in and before the standard process for generating file names is run.	Generate or change the name of the original file when creating a new version of the document information record.

Table 10.3 Available Methods, Time of Execution, and Example Usage for BAdI DOCUMENT_FILES01 (Cont.)

10.1.4 BAdI DOCUMENT_STORAGE01 - Transport of Original Application Files

BAdI DOCUMENT_STORAGE01 lets you perform additional checks or actions before or after check in/check out of an original application files that are associated to the document information record.

Available methods, time of execution, and example usage for this BAdI are outlined in Table 10.4.

Method	Time Of Execution	Example Usage
Before_Checkin	Before physical check-in of an original application file.	Compress the original file being checked in.
After_Checkin	After physical checkin of an original application file.	Automatically set the status of the document information record to a review state, such as pending review. Setting this status may trigger a review workflow.

Table 10.4 Available Methods, Time of Execution, and Example Usage for BAdI DOCUMENT_STORAGE01

Method	Time Of Execution	Example Usage
Before_Checkout	Before physical checkout of an original application file when displaying, changing or copying the file. This is also executed for original files that are not checked in.	Adjust the file name before it reaches the frontend computer.
Before_List_Storagecat	Before the display of the possible storage categories when checking in an original file.	Filter the list of possible storage categories based on the user's location.

Table 10.4 Available Methods, Time of Execution, and Example Usage for BAdI DOCUMENT_STORAGE01 (Cont.)

10.1.5 BAdI DOCUMENT_STATUS01 - Status checks

Using BAdI DOCUMENT_STATUS01, you can trigger additional actions or perform specifics system checks before or after the status of the document information record is set.

Available methods, time of execution, and example usage for this BAdI are outlined in Table 10.5.

Method	Time Of Execution	Example Usage
After_Change_Status	After every status change.	Execute a custom report when a document information record reaches a status of "Released." The report output is then linked to the document information record.
Before_List_Status	Before the list of possible statuses is displayed.	Complete additional checks beyond standard configuration for which statuses are possible and selectable by users.

Table 10.5 Available Methods, Time of Execution, and Example Usage for BAdI DOCUMENT_STATUS01

10.1.6 BAdI DOCUMENT_MAN02 - Document Exits and Menu Enhancements

BAdI DOCUMENT_MAN02 lets you check menu enhancements at the point in time of process after input (PAI).

Checks are executed with the following Transactions:

- Create document (CV01N)
- Change document (CV02N)
- Display document (CV03N)

Available methods, time of execution, and example usage for this BAdI are outlined in Table 10.6.

Interface	Time Of Execution	Example Usage
D100_Before_PAI	Before the actual PAI of screen 100	Additional checks when selecting a function in DMS.
D101_Before_PAI	Before the actual PAI of screen 101	Additional checks when selecting a function in DMS.
D100_PAI_CU1	PAI for menu enhancement 1 (+D100_CU1) screen 100	Processing of menu enhancements.
D100_PAI_CU2	PAI for menu enhancement 1 (+D100_CU2) screen 100	Processing of menu enhancements.
D100_PAI_CU3	PAI for menu enhancement 1 (+D100_CU3) screen 100	Processing of menu enhancements.
D100_PAI_CU1	PAI for menu enhancement 1 (+D100_CU1) screen 101	Processing of menu enhancements.
D101_PAI_CU2	PAI for menu enhancement 1 (+D100_CU2) screen 101	Processing of menu enhancements.
D101_PAI_CU3	PAI for menu enhancement 1 (+D100_CU3) screen 101	Processing of menu enhancements.

Table 10.6 Available Methods, Time of Execution, and Example Usage for BAdI DOCUMENT_MAN02

10.1.7 BAdI DOCUMENT_NUMBER01 - Checking the Attributes of the Document Key

Using BAdI DOCUMENT_NUMBER01, you can perform additional checks on key attributes associated with the document information record. This includes checks for the document number, document version, document version, and getting the next and last version.

Available methods, time of execution, and example usage for this BAdI are outlined in Table 10.7.

Interface	Time Of Execution	Example Usage
DOCNUMBER_Check	Before standard checks are carried out by SAP DMS.	Carry out an additional check for the assignment of a document number.
DOCVERSION_Check	Before standard checks are carried out by SAP DMS.	Carry out an additional check for the assignment of a document version.
DOCPART_Check	Before standard checks are carried out by SAP DMS.	Carry out an additional check for the assignment of a document part.
DOCVERSION_Get_Next	When creating a new version of a document.	Get the next version of a document information record. Beyond basic determination, this may include additional rules for determination.
DOCVERSION_Get_Last	When creating a new version of a document.	Determine the last version of a document information record.

Table 10.7 Available Methods, Time of Execution, and Example Usage for BAdI DOCUMENT_NUMBER01

10.1.8 BAdI: DOCUMENT_PROC01 - Filter for DMS Processes

BAdI DOCUMENT_PROC01 lets you limit what processes are listed when the Processes button is used in Transaction Find Document (CV04N). A process is defined as an action that you can take on a selected set of document information records returned through executing of the Find Document transaction. An example process would be to set the deletion indicator on execution of the process for the selected document information records.

Available methods, time of execution, and example usage for BAdI DOCUMENT_ PROC01 are outlined in Table 10.8.

Interface	Time Of Execution	Example Usage
Before_List_Process	Before displaying a list of processes.	Based on the user's location, only list certain processes that can be executed.
Before_List_Status	Not implemented in current releases.	N/A

Table 10.8 Available Methods, Time of Execution, and Example Usage for BAdI DOCUMENT_ PROC01

10.1.9 BAdI DOCUMENT_WEB01- Enhancements for the DMS@Web Scenarios

You can use BAdI DOCUMENT_WEB01, to filter original files and to retrieve the URL for checkout of an original file.

Available methods, time of execution, and example usage for this BAdI are outlined in Table 10.9.

Interface	Time Of Execution	Example Usage
Filter_Files	Before transferring document data to the Internet Transaction Server (ITS).	Checks of original application files in the Web scenario.
Get_URL	-	Determine URL for checkout in the Web.

Table 10.9 Available Methods, Time of Execution, and Example Usage for BAdI DOCUMENT_ WEB01

10.1.10 BAdI DOCUMENT_OFFINTEGR01 - Enhancements for Microsoft Office Integration

Using BAdI DOCUMENT_OFFINTEGR01, you can control or enhance the Microsoft Office integration that is used to display or change original files.

Available methods, time of execution, and example usage of this BAdI are outlined in Table 10.10.

Interface	Time Of Execution	Example Usage
Edit_Link_Items	Before data is transferred from SAP to the Microsoft Office application. (Word, Excel, etc.)	Transfer additional data from the SAP system to the Microsoft Office application.
After_Open	After opening an original application file in a Microsoft Office application.	When viewing, set an additional attribute in the document information record that lists information such as the date and time the file was opened.
Read_Class	When reading the classification of the Microsoft Office integration.	N/A
Edit_Form_Items	After opening the Microsoft Office application, to transfer data from the SAP system to the Microsoft Office application.	Transfer additional data from a material master or other object that is related to the document information record.

Table 10.10 Available Methods, Time of Execution, and Example Usage for BAdI DOCUMENT_OFFINTEGR01

10.1.11 BAdI DOCUMENT_ECL01 - Displaying Original Application Files with the Viewer

With BAdI DOCUMENT_ECL01, in connection with using the SAP ECL viewer and the viewer's stamping functionality, you can add additional information from the document information record to the stamp.

Also, in the viewer's comparison tool, you can restrict or preselect which files should be available for comparison.

Available methods, time of execution, and example usage for this BAdI are outlined in Table 10.11.

Interface	Time Of Execution	Example Usage
Show_Doc_Meta_Data	Before stamping of viewable file.	Transfer additional information from the document information record to be included in the stamping of a viewable file.
Before_List_Docs_To_Add	Before generating the selection list in the Select Original dialog box.	Based on business rules, preselect or restrict which documents are added to the Select Original dialog box.

Table 10.11 Available Methods, Time of Execution, and Example Usage for BAdI DOCUMENT_ECL01

10.1.12 BAdI CONVERTER_MAIN01 - Exits During Conversion

Using BAdI CONVERTER_MAIN01, after a conversion process, you can update or apply additional actions such as changing data before the results of the conversion process are stored.

Available methods, time of execution, and example usage for this BAdI are outlined in Table 10.12.

Interface	Time Of Execution	Example Usage
Checkin_Change_WS_Application	After the conversion process has run.	Change the workstation application associated to the original file before check in.
Checkin_Before_Checkin	After the conversion process has run.	Change the description, storage category, or other data element before check in of file.
Checkin_After_Checkin	After the conversion process has run.	Delete files after check in.

Table 10.12 Available Methods, Time of Execution, and Example Usage for BAdI CONVERTER_MAIN01

10.2   User Exits Available In SAP DMS

In this chapter, greater emphasis is placed on BAdIs than user exits. This is because most SAP DMS enhancements can be carried out using one of the BAdIs. However, a number of useful user exits exist, specifically in the area of document distribution. As you can see in Table 10.13, user exits CVDI0001 through CVDI0020 are all related to document distribution. Therefore, these can be used when enhancing this functionality. As an example, you can use user exit CVDI0003 to determine which original files should be sent with a distribution order.

Exit	Description
CV000001	Check in enhancement for document management
CV110001	DMS: Enhancements for DMS dialog
CVDI0001	User exit: Document Distribution (DDS) - save recipient list
CVDI0002	User exit: DDS - Modify initial values for screen 100
CVDI0003	User exit: DDS - Determine original
CVDI0004	User exit: DDS - Determine document part and version
CVDI0005	User exit: DDS - Create distribution order
CVDI0006	User exit: DDS - Check part order
CVDI0007	User exit: DDS - Create initial order
CVDI0008	User exit: DDS - Determine context
CVDI0009	User exit: DDS - Access to ITS
CVDI0010	User exit: DDS - Determine workstation application
CVDI0011	User exit: DDS: ITS access to all distribution packages
CVDI0020	User exit for distributing originals
CVDS0001	User exit for ALE DMS (DOCMAS)

Table 10.13   Available SAP DMS User Exits

10.3   Summary

In this chapter, we reviewed the use of SAP BAdIs and user exits. We defined the methods, time of execution, and example usage for each BAdI and looked at the available, related user exists. By utilizing BAdIs or user exits, you can enhance the system to include functionality that is not delivered through standard IMG configuration. It is often the case during projects that a business requirement will go beyond the standard configuration. When this occurs, you can use the information in this chapter to develop a solution.

In the next chapter, we will briefly review what we have covered in this book. In addition, we will address the future of SAP DMS.

This chapter will review what you've learned throughout this book and the future of SAP DMS.

11   Conclusion

Congratulations on arriving at the conclusion of this book. At this point, you have spent a good deal of time studying and learning about SAP DMS. In this chapter, we'll provide you with a chapter-by-chapter review of what you have learned by reading this book, with brief highlights and key points for each chapter. At the end of the chapter, we'll give you an idea of what SAP DMS might look like in the future.

11.1   SAP DMS: Now You Know It

In this section, we will briefly recap what you have learned in each chapter of this book.

11.1.1   Introduction

After reading through Chapter 1, Introduction, you developed the skills to evaluate whether SAP DMS is right for you, and what SAP DMS can offer your business. From this introduction, you should understand what SAP DMS is: an enterprise document management system available in your base SAP system. We took a look at some of the benefits of implementing SAP DMS, including secure storage for documents, full text search across documents, and the ability to classify documents for searching. After learning about SAP DMS benefits, you learned how to judge the complexity of your project by looking at the volume of different types of documents you plan to manage with SAP DMS, making sure to take the types of resources required for a project into consideration. You also learned how to use this book: as a beginner you should start from the simple chapters and move on to the more complex; as an advanced user, you can go through the book in any order that meets your needs. Finally, you learned about the availability of SAP DMS across different releases.

11.1.2   Questions to Answer before Starting Your SAP DMS Project

In Chapter 2, Questions to Answer before Starting Your SAP DMS Project, you learned that document management is not simply about storing files, but that instead it's important to answer key questions about your SAP DMS project before moving on to actual system activities. This way you have a firm idea of the goals you want to achieve with SAP DMS. In this chapter, you reviewed which documents should be defined and managed in SAP DMS. You also considered how you want to search for documents and what attributes are necessary to meet these requirements. You learned that structure and attributes must exist on which you can search to find documents. Reading this chapter, you obtained the skills and insight to start defining your requirements so that when you learned the basic functions and configuration activities you were able to tailor the system to your requirements.

11.1.3   SAP DMS Step-by-Step Instructions

In Chapter 3, SAP DMS Step-by-Step Instructions, you learned how to execute the basic SAP DMS transactions. This includes the transactions to create, change, and display document information records. You also learned about additional transactions to execute document searches, classification searches, and you reviewed the product structure browser. Knowledge of these items is helpful before moving on to the configuration activity. As an example, by learning how to create a document information record, you learn about document types, additional attributes, and statuses. These are all items that can be configured and knowing how they relate to other items in the system makes the configuration activity much clearer to you.

11.1.4   Configuring SAP DMS

Beyond learning how to operate the basic transactions of SAP DMS, Chapter 4, Configuring SAP DMS, covered the next most important topic, configuration. Configuration lets you set up SAP DMS to meet your business requirements. With the configuration items complete, you were able to use the SAP DMS system and move on to additional topics such as defining your security requirements, or enhancing the system through the use of SAP-provide BAdIs.

11.1.5 Infrastructure Requirements

In Chapter 5, Infrastructure Requirements, you learned about the different infrastructure pieces available to support your SAP DMS projects. The infrastructure pieces are underlying system elements that make SAP DMS possible, but are invisible to the user. They include the content, cache, TREX, and conversion servers. Each infrastructure piece fulfills a unique requirement important for an SAP DMS system. You also learned about different architecture options. A simple architecture would involve a single content server that covers all of your requirements. If you have a more complex environment with people at multiple locations accessing and creating data, you can install multiple content and cache servers, creating a more complex environment. What a complex environment ultimately looks like depends on the number of users, and locations being served, and how your wide area network is structured.

11.1.6 SAP DMS Security

At the beginning of Chapter 6, SAP DMS Security, you learned about questions to consider when defining your SAP DMS security scheme. These helped you understand and define your security requirements. You also learned about the different authorization objects that SAP provides for creating a security scheme. Finally, there was discussion of how to use a specific BAdI to create a customer-specific authorization check using ABAP.

11.1.7 Frontends to SAP DMS

In Chapter 7, Frontends to SAP DMS, you learned about three different frontends: Web Documents, Easy DMS, and the SAP DMS Portal iView. Frontends are important because they offer a different user experience, possibly simpler, for accessing and executing SAP DMS functionalities than using the SAP GUI. Users of these frontends might include persons that are classified as consumers of information. They are individuals who are looking for easy ways to get at the information in SAP DMS, rather than creating and changing information in the system. The frontend interfaces work using the same configuration as SAP DMS; therefore, when you have your base SAP DMS configuration working in the SAP GUI, you can start working with the different frontends to see if the user experience is appropriate for you and your users.

11.1.8   Integrating a CAD System to SAP DMS

In Chapter 8, Integrating a CAD System to SAP DMS, you learned that, yes, it is possible to integrate your CAD system to SAP DMS! CAD systems you can integrate include AutoCAD, CATIA, UG NX, and Pro/Engineer. You also saw some of the benefits of integrating a CAD system to SAP, including secure data storage, the ability to execute SAP DMS transactions directly from a CAD system, and the ability to use engineering change management tools to control updates to CAD data. You also learned about the CAD Desktop, which is the tool provide by SAP for management of CAD data within the SAP GUI. Finally, you walked through a sample scenario to learn about the steps involved in working with a CAD integration.

11.1.9   Simple Document Approval Process using SAP Workflow

In Chapter 9, Simple Document Approval Process Using SAP Workflow, you learned how to create a basic document approval workflow so that you can build on this example to create more complex workflows. The concepts covered included how to build a workflow definition, what triggering events and container elements are, and how to activate and test your workflow after it has been built. The combination of SAP DMS and SAP Workflow can be powerful in that it lets you automate approval/review processes and an unlimited number of additional business processes.

11.1.10   SAP DMS BAdIs and User Exits

Chapter 10, SAP DMS BAdIs and User Exists, taught you about going beyond basic SAP DMS configuration by using BAdIs and user exits provided by SAP to enhance SAP DMS. You learned about twelve different BAdIs, and how and why they are superior to user exits. For each BAdI, you learned about the different methods, time of execution, and saw an example of usage. Although BAdIs typically address most requirements, a number of helpful user exits also exist for document distribution and ALE.

11.2   The Future of SAP DMS

Looking into the SAP crystal ball can be difficult. However, with SAP DMS, there are some clues as to where it will head in the future. One thing you can look for are additional frontends to SAP DMS to further enhance the user experience. Users are always looking for easier ways to get documents and data stored into the SAP system and likely, SAP DMS will become more integrated into applications, such as the Microsoft Office suite. This gives users the ability to interact with SAP DMS directly from the applications they use to create data, lowering the number of clicks needed to store data, and moving further away from a traditional GUI interface. Fewer clicks make users feel less like they are working with an SAP system, and as a result, the acceptance level goes up.

11.3   Summary

In this chapter, we provided you with a look back on what you have learned by reading this book, and how it fits into the big picture of your projects. We have covered a lot of material on different subjects and topics; if you have judiciously studied the content of this book, you now have all of the tools you need to use and configure SAP DMS.

We hope that you have enjoyed reading and have gained useful insight into SAP DMS and why it is an important tool for you and your organization, and how to put this tool to use.

Appendices

This chapter covers terminology and definitions for the terms most frequently used in SAP DMS.

A   Glossary

It is important to know the terminology used in SAP DMS and will be helpful as you work through your SAP DMS project. In this appendix, we therefore provide you with terminology definitions for terms that are used most frequently.

Authorization group   An authorization group is used, among other options, to control access to documents. It consists of a four character alphanumeric identifier. If an authorization group is assigned to a document information record, the user must have this authorization group in their security profile.

Cache server   The cache server is a designated server that keeps a cached copy of original files as they are pulled for viewing or change. It is usually located at a remote location that does not have a content server. Requests from the remote location to view documents will go first to the cache server and then to the content server where the original file is located. The goal is to help reduce network usage.

CAD interface   A CAD interface allows you to interface a CAD system directly to the SAP DMS system. For example, SAP offers CAD interfaces to interface AutoCAD, UG, CATIA, and Pro/E directly to SAP DMS. Using these interfaces, certain SAP DMS functions can be carried out directly in the CAD system.

CAD indicator   The CAD indicator is located on a document information record to show whether a document information record has been created or changed through a CAD interface to SAP DMS.

Change number   A change number is an engineering change master or engineering change request/order used to control the creation and change of document information records.

Content server   A content server stores original files that are checked into the SAP DMS system. This server is separate from the main SAP DMS system. There can be one or many content servers associated with an instance of SAP DMS.

Content version   If configured, the SAP DMS system will store a copy of the original file each time it is stored back in the system after being checked out. This copy of the original file is referred to as a content version.

Conversion server   The conversion server is a dedicated server that converts original files stored with a document information record into a neutral format such as TIF or PDF. A conversion can be triggered based on a status change. The conversion processes are controlled through IMG configuration.

Deletion indicator   The deletion indicator on a document information record indicates whether the document information record should be deleted from the system. Deletion is carried out through program MCDOKDEL.

Document description   A document description describes the document that is being stored. It consists of 40 characters.

Document distribution   A document distribution is a system used to distribute documents from the document management system. Documents are distributed according to different criteria (for example, communication type, and context).

Document information record   The document information record is the record in the SAP DMS system that contains attributes that describe the original file being stored. Attributes include owner, status, short description, authorization group, and attributes that are defined through configuration.

Document key   The document key consists of four elements:

▶ Document number

▶ Document type

▶ Document part

▶ Document version

These four elements together make up the document key. For example: 1000000/DRW/000/00.

Document number   The document number is a unique id for each document information record. It can be internally or externally generated, and can consist of numbers or a combination of numbers and letters. It is an element of the document key. Some examples include:

▶ Numeric: 10000003236

▶ Alphanumeric: Spec10001

▶ Alpha: SpecF150

Document owner   The document owner is the person who is responsible for the document information record. At initial creation, the name of the creator is placed into the field USER on the document information record. When a document is updated, the name in the USER field is updated with the name of the individual making the change.

Document part   Document part is a section of a document that is maintained as an independent document. Design departments, for example, can use document parts to divide large documents, such as design drawings, into pages. It is an element of the document key.

Document status   The document status identifies where in its lifecycle a document information record is at. Example statuses include "In-Work" and "Released." The document status controls items such as security, and triggers processes such as automated document conversions.

Document structure indicator   The document structure indicator specifies whether the document information record has an associated document structure. A document structure is similar to a BOM. Functions to process the document structure can be accessed under the "Environment" menu item in the document information record.

Document type   The document type is a high-level categorization of a group of documents. It consists of a three character alphanumeric identifier. It is an element of the document key. An example of a document type is DRW.

Document version   The document version is a number or letter that identifies a document's version. It is an element of the document key.

ECL viewer   The ECL viewer is provided by SAP for viewing a variety of 2-D and 3-D formats. Using the viewer for a specific file format is controlled through IMG configuration.

Frontend type   Frontend types, also called data carriers, are defined through IMG configuration. The data carrier controls how original files will be processed on a local machine. This concept is important when you go through the IMG activity "Define Workstation Application." When defining how an application should start for an original file, this definition is associated to a data carrier.

Index server   The index server is a dedicated server that indexes documents stored in a content server for the full text search functionality to work.

Lab office   The lab office is the design office, laboratory, or location that is responsible for the document being stored. Values for lab office are controlled through material master configuration.

Neutral file   A neutral file is generated out of an automated conversion process. Conversion takes place on a conversion server. This is usually a TIF or PDF file.

Object links   Through the OBJECT LINKS tab in the document information record, you can link a document information record to many other objects in the SAP system. This is important because it provides a way to link supporting documentation to these other objects. For example, let's say that a company stored specification using SAP DMS. Through object linking, it is possible to link the specifications to related material masters.

Original file   An original file is an application file that is associated to a document information record. One or many original files can be attached to a document information record.

Redline and markup   Redline and markup is the process of using the redlining and markup tools in the ECL Viewer to make annotations to a file that is stored using SAP DMS. Redline and markup can occur on file formats such as TIF and PDF.

Revision   A revision is a single-character field that identifies the revision of a document. The REVISION field is available only when using a change number associated to the document information record.

Status network   The status network is the lifecycle of the document information record. An example status network would be as follows: A document information record starts in the status of "In-Work." It then can be set to a status of "Being Checked." From the "Being Checked" status it can be set to "Released," or it can go back to "In-Work." Through IMG configuration, you can build a status network for each document type.

Status log   The status log is a record of when a status was set on a document information record. It also includes a short comment from the user setting the status. This comment can be configured to be mandatory, optional, or bypassed, based on IMG configuration.

Workstation application   A workstation application is the application that is defined to start when viewing or changing an original file associated to a document information record.

B Review of Menu Items

This appendix provides you with an overview of the menu options in SAP DMS transactions (as circled in Figure B.1), and descriptions for each of the menu items that appear below each option.

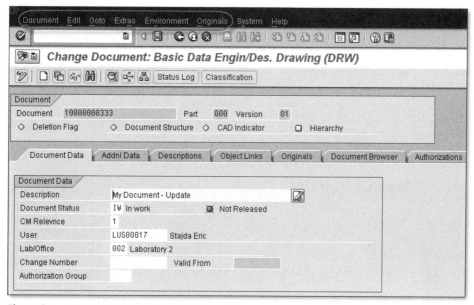

Figure B.1 Menu Options in SAP DMS Transactions

B.1 Menu Option Document

Menu Item	Description
Other Document	Open another document information record.
Create	Create a new document information record.
Change	If in display mode, switch to change mode.
Display	If in change mode, switch to display mode.
Find	Open the find document transaction (Transaction CV04N).

Menu Item	Description
New Version	Create a new version of the current document information record.
Save	Save the document information record.
Change Deletion Ind.	Set the deletion indicator on the document information record. Actual deletion of document information record is carried out through program MCDOKDEL.
Exit	Exit the current transaction.

B.2   Menu Option Edit

Menu Item	Description
Cancel	Cancel the transaction.

B.3   Menu Option Goto

Menu Item	Description
Messages	Display messages.
Back	Back out of the transaction.

B.4   Menu Option Extras

Menu Item	Description
Classification	Display the classification information for the active document information record.
Versions	Display a list of versions for the active document information record.
Document Parts	Display a list of document parts for the active document information record.
Sequence of Sources	Show the sequence of sources, or from which document information record the active document information record was created.

Menu Item	Description
Hierarchy	If the document information record belongs to a hierarchy, display the report showing the document hierarchy.
Status Network	Display the status network for the active document information record.
Status Log	Display the status log for the active document information record.
Settings	Set a working directory for an application.
Change Front End Type	Change the frontend type. This is important when you are working on a client that is not Windows-based, such as a UNIX client. The frontend type controls how applications are launched when displaying or changing original files.

B.5   Menu Option Environment

Menu Item	Description
Display Changes	Display the change history report for the active document information record.
Revision Levels	Display the revision levels for the active document information record.
Document Where Used	Excute a where-used report to check whether the document is used in a document structure.
Product Structure	Open the product structure browser with the context of the active document information record.
Document Structure	Execute functions related to document structures.
Document Distribution	Execute functions related to document distribution.
Digitial Signatures	Display digital signatures associated with the active document information record.
Check In Archive	Store and associate an original file using the archive link functionality.
Display From Archive	Display an original file that was associated to the active document information record through an archive link.
Copy From Archive	Copy a document associated to the active document information record from an archive link.

B.6   Menu Option Originals

Menu Item	Description
Check In Original	Check in an original file.
Check In As	Check in an original file to a specific storage category.
Check In As New Version	Check in an original file as a new content version.
Process Under	Check out an original file to a location on a local machine.
Copy To	Copy an original file to a location on a local machine. This is accomplished without checking out the file.
Reset Check-Out	Cancel the checking out of a file. This is often helpful if a local file has been corrupted after check out and you want to return to the previously stored copy.

B.7   Additional Resources

For additional help on any of the menu items mention in this appendix, SAP Help provides a great deal of information. SAP Help can be accessed at *http://help.sap.com*.

You can find SAP DMS-specific help under the heading SAP ERP CENTRAL COMPONENT.

C   The Author

Eric Stajda is Senior Consultant at LeverX specializing in the area of SAP PLM. He has helped customers find and implement solutions in a variety of industries, including automotive, high-tech, pharmaceuticals, discrete manufacturing, and oil and gas. Most recently, he has been developing and deploying rapid prototyping techniques to help customers implement SAP PLM functionalities, including SAP DMS, in a faster, more cost efficient manner. He is a regular speaker at SAP conferences, including ASUG, SAP Insider, and SAPPHIRE. He resides in the Detroit area, with his wife, Liz.

Please send email inquiries to: *eric@sap-plm.com*.

Linkedin Profile: *http://www.linkedin.com/in/estajda*.

Index

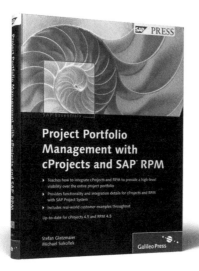

Teaches how to integrate cProjects and RPM
to provide a high-level visibility over the entire
project portfolio

Provides functionality and integration details for
cProjects and RPM with SAP Project System

Includes real-world customer examples
throughout

Up-to-date for cProjects 4.5 and RPM 4.5

Stefan Glatzmaier, Michael Sokollek

Project Portfolio Management with SAP RPM and cProjects

SAP PRESS Essentials 49

This essentials guide introduces and teaches users how to integrate and
use project portfolio management with SAP to support their business
processes. The book focuses on cProjects and SAP RPM, as well as the
integration with SAP Project System. With real-life examples, this book
uses examples to illustrate specific solution options and projects. The
main chapters are based on the actual business processes in an enterprise
and contain industry-specific recommendations. The book is based on
the latest releases, and is a must-have addition to any SAP library.

approx. 356 pp., 68,– Euro / US$ 85
ISBN 978-1-59229-224-0, Dec 2008

>> www.sap-press.de/1838

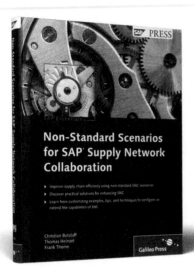

Improve supply chain efficiency using non-standard SNC scenarios

Discover practical solutions for enhancing SNC

Learn from customizing examples, tips, and techniques to configure or extend the capabilities of SNC

Christian Butzlaff, Thomas Heinzel, Frank Thome

Non-Standard Scenarios for SAP Supply Network Collaboration

SAP PRESS Essentials 43

This Essentials is a detailed guide for those needing unique and new scenarios to maximize their SNC solution. Based on SAP SNC 5.1, it focuses on insightful, new information usually only available from highly experienced consultants or SAP development, such as enhanced business scenarios, and notification and authorization enhancements. The book begins with a concise review of SNC, its architecture, and standard scenarios, and then quickly moves on to the non-standard scenarios and other techniques for enhancing and customizing SAP SNC.

approx. 200 pp., 68,– Euro / US$ 85
ISBN 978-1-59229-195-3, Jan 2009

>> www.sap-press.de/1741

Master real-life business processes and the structuringof plant maintenance technical systems

Discover tips and tricks for implementing daily operations

Explore interfaces, reporting, and new EAM technologies – MAM, RFID, Enterprise SOA, NetWeaver Portal, and more

Karl Liebstückel

SAP Enterprise Asset Management

This is a must-have guide for anyone interested in learning about the implementation and customization of SAP EAM. Consultants, managers, and administrators will learn about the plant maintenance process, how to evaluate which processes work best for them, and then go on to review the actual configuration steps of these processes. This book includes practical tips and best practices for implementation projects. The companion DVD contains examples, practice tests, presentations, and more. This book is up-to-date for SAP ERP 6.0.

552 pp., 2008, with CD, 69,95 Euro / US$ 69.95
ISBN 978-1-59229-150-2

>> www.sap-press.de/1528

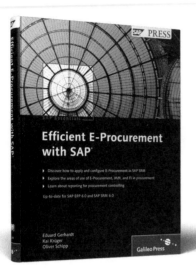

Learn how to use E-Procurement effectively with other SAP components, including MM and Financials

Explore the implementation processes to ensure an effective implementation

Find out how to optimize your procurement processes, reduce ordering costs, decentralize purchase orders, and more

Up-to-date for SAP ERP 6.0

Eduard Gerhardt, Kai Krüger, Oliver Schipp

Efficient E-Procurement with SAP

SAP PRESS Essentials 47

This book describes how to carry out procurement processes and map these processes in the SAP system, using the E-Procurement solution. Readers will learn which SAP tool is best suited for which requirement in purchasing and procurement, and which usage options these tools provide. Above all, readers will get to know how they can use E-Procurement in order to optimize their own procurement processes, reduce ordering costs, decentralize purchase orders, and reduce the Purchasing department workload.

approx. 201 pp., 68,– Euro / US$ 85
ISBN 978-1-59229-209-7, Oct 2008

>> www.sap-press.de/1789

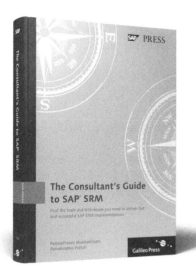

Find the tools and techniques you need
to deliver fast and successful SAP SRM
implementations

PadmaPrasad Munirathinam, Ramakrishna Potluri

Consultant's Guide to SAP SRM

**Find the tools and techniques you need to deliver fast and successful SAP SRM
implementations**

Consultants hold many roles during an SAP implementation, from business consultant
during the blueprint phase, and product specialist (techno-functional expert) during the
realization phase, to trainer after go-live. This book provides all of the information a
consultant needs to hold these roles effectively and to ensure that they are delivering the
most value to their customers.

Based on SAP SRM 6.0, the book targets the specific needs of consultants and provides a
comprehensive guide to implementing SAP SRM and purchasing best practices. Each
chapter covers a specific process of supplier relationship management, ensuring that
implementation teams can utilize their time efficiently. Going beyond standard SRM
scenarios, the book arms consultants with practical tips for enabling complex customer
requirements, and provides insightful troubleshooting tips and techniques.

512 pp., 2008, 79,95 Euro / US$ 79.95
ISBN 978-1-59229-154-0

>> www.sap-press.de/1558

Provides a comprehensive overview of the entire delivery process

Teaches functions, processes, and customization

Covers dangerous goods management, availability checks, user exits, and much more

Othmar Gau

Transportation Management with SAP LES

This in-depth reference provides readers with practical and detailed knowledge on all aspects of shipping and transportation with SAP Logistics Execution System (LES). Using this book, employees in the warehouse and shipping departments, as well as consultants, can benefit from proven best practices for working successfully with the Transportation Management module. The author describes the entire shipping and delivery process, from the creation of a delivery in the SAP system, to mapping the internal supply chain, and from transportation planning to invoicing and settlement with forwarding agencies – and everything in between. Plus, readers also learn how to master system configuration, and much more.

574 pp., 2008, 79,95 Euro / US$ 79.95
ISBN 978-1-59229-169-4

>> www.sap-press.de/1594

Interested in reading more?

Please visit our Web site for all
new book releases from SAP PRESS.

www.sap-press.com